Current
CONTROVERSIES

Medical Ethics

Other Books in the Current Controversies Series

Medical Ethics

Noël Merino, Book Editor

GREENHAVEN PRESS
A part of Gale, Cengage Learning

GALE
CENGAGE Learning·

Farmington Hills, Mich • San Francisco • New York • Waterville, Maine
Meriden, Conn • Mason, Ohio • Chicago

Patricia Coryell, *Vice President & Publisher, New Products & GVRL*
Douglas Dentino, *Manager, New Products*
Judy Galens, *Aquisitions Editor*

For more information, contact:
Greenhaven Press
27500 Drake Rd.
Farmington Hills, MI 48331-3535
Or you can visit our Internet site at gale.cengage.com

For product information and technology assistance, contact us at

Gale Customer Support, 1-800-877-4253
For permission to use material from this text or product, submit all requests online at
www.cengage.com/permissions

Further permissions questions can be emailed to permissionrequest@cengage.com

Articles in Greenhaven Press anthologies are often edited for length to meet page requirements. In addition, original titles of these works are changed to clearly present the main thesis and to explicitly indicate the author's opinion. Every effort is made to ensure that Greenhaven Press accurately reflects the original intent of the authors. Every effort has been made to trace the owners of copyrighted material.

Cover image © Andy Dean Photography/Shutterstock.com.

LIBRARY OF CONGRESS CATALOGING-IN-PUBLICATION DATA

Medical ethics / Noël Merino, book editor.
   pages cm. -- (Current controversies)
  Includes bibliographical references and index.
  ISBN 978-0-7377-7221-0 (hardback) -- ISBN 978-0-7377-7222-7 (paperback)
  1. Medical ethics. 2. Medical ethics--United States. I. Merino, Noël, editor.
  R724.M292742 2015
  174.2--dc23
                                         2014044392

Printed in the United States of America
1 2 3 4 5 6 7 19 18 17 16 15

Contents

Chapter 1: What Ethics Should Guide the Health-Care System?

A clear majority of Americans now disapprove of the Affordable Care Act (ACA), primarily due to disapproval of government interference in mandating health insurance. Another factor is the impact the law has had on those Americans who were forced to get new insurance policies, because their previous ones did not meet the minimum standards set by the ACA.

The US health-care system is not working and the only long-term solution to the crisis is a single-payer national health-care program for all Americans. Such a system would be good for Americans, good for businesses, and good for our overall economy.

Health care is not a right, and therefore it is morally wrong for government to force people to pay for other people's medical care. Those who cannot pay should rely on voluntary charity rather than tax-payer assistance.

In the long term, the United States cannot afford to pay for a publicly financed health-care system, because such a system fosters perverse incentives, such as the incentive to work less and use more health care than necessary. As such, the Affordable Care Act will ultimately lead the country to bankruptcy faster than would happen otherwise.

Chapter 2: What Ethics Should Guide Organ Transplants?

Chapter 3: Are Reproductive Technologies Ethical?

New reproductive technologies raise a variety of issues regarding risks, bioethical responsibility, the commercialization of fertility, and social class. It is imperative that we confront these issues as advances in assisted reproduction technologies continue to occur.

Yes: Reproductive Technologies Are Ethical

No: Reproductive Technologies Are Not Always Ethical

The ever-increasing likelihood of being able to completely genetically engineer children, such as that depicted in the 1997 film *Gattaca*, is leading to disturbing ethical claims about parenthood and perfection. The fundamental flaw with the mindset in *Gattaca* is that it fails to recognize the value of human difference.

Chapter 4: Is It Ethical for Medical Professionals to End Life?

The majority of Americans believe there are some situations in which a patient should be allowed to die, but they are split on whether a physician should be allowed to help. While this majority has remained fairly steady over the years, a growing minority—nearly a third of respondents—says that medical professionals should do everything possible to save a patient's life.

Yes: It Is Ethical for Medical Professionals to End Life

No: It Is Not Ethical for Medical Professionals to End Life

The trend toward forcing medical professionals to take part in life-ending procedures, such as aid in dying and abortion, violates the Hippocratic Oath, and thus doctors need strong laws enacted that protect their medical conscience.

Foreword

By definition, controversies are "discussions of questions in which opposing opinions clash" (*Webster's Twentieth Century Dictionary Unabridged*). Few would deny that controversies are a pervasive part of the human condition and exist on virtually every level of human enterprise. Controversies transpire between individuals and among groups, within nations and between nations. Controversies supply the grist necessary for progress by providing challenges and challengers to the status quo. They also create atmospheres where strife and warfare can flourish. A world without controversies would be a peaceful world; but it also would be, by and large, static and prosaic.

The Series' Purpose

The purpose of the Current Controversies series is to explore many of the social, political, and economic controversies dominating the national and international scenes today. Titles selected for inclusion in the series are highly focused and specific. For example, from the larger category of criminal justice, Current Controversies deals with specific topics such as police brutality, gun control, white collar crime, and others. The debates in Current Controversies also are presented in a useful, timeless fashion. Articles and book excerpts included in each title are selected if they contribute valuable, long-range ideas to the overall debate. And wherever possible, current information is enhanced with historical documents and other relevant materials. Thus, while individual titles are current in focus, every effort is made to ensure that they will not become quickly outdated. Books in the Current Controversies series will remain important resources for librarians, teachers, and students for many years.

In addition to keeping the titles focused and specific, great care is taken in the editorial format of each book in the series. Book introductions and chapter prefaces are offered to provide background material for readers. Chapters are organized around several key questions that are answered with diverse opinions representing all points on the political spectrum. Materials in each chapter include opinions in which authors clearly disagree as well as alternative opinions in which authors may agree on a broader issue but disagree on the possible solutions. In this way, the content of each volume in Current Controversies mirrors the mosaic of opinions encountered in society. Readers will quickly realize that there are many viable answers to these complex issues. By questioning each author's conclusions, students and casual readers can begin to develop the critical thinking skills so important to evaluating opinionated material.

Current Controversies is also ideal for controlled research. Each anthology in the series is composed of primary sources taken from a wide gamut of informational categories including periodicals, newspapers, books, US and foreign government documents, and the publications of private and public organizations. Readers will find factual support for reports, debates, and research papers covering all areas of important issues. In addition, an annotated table of contents, an index, a book and periodical bibliography, and a list of organizations to contact are included in each book to expedite further research.

Perhaps more than ever before in history, people are confronted with diverse and contradictory information. During the Persian Gulf War, for example, the public was not only treated to minute-to-minute coverage of the war, it was also inundated with critiques of the coverage and countless analyses of the factors motivating US involvement. Being able to sort through the plethora of opinions accompanying today's major issues, and to draw one's own conclusions, can be a complicated and frustrating struggle. It is the editors' hope that Current Controversies will help readers with this struggle.

Introduction

> *"Even where agreement can be found on broad ethical principles, just how they apply to various medical practices is far from resolved."*

Ethics can be defined as the system of values that governs behavior. Medical ethics is the field of ethics that involves the values and responsibilities within the field of medicine. To say that a certain medical practice is ethical is to say that it aligns with the right values. To deem a certain practice unethical is to say that it does not comport with the right values. There is no consensus on the medical ethics that ought to guide medical professionals, which is clear by looking at the evolving nature of the Hippocratic Oath and the lack of any common system of accepted ethical medical practices.

Hippocrates was an ancient Greek physician born in the fifth century BC. The Hippocratic Corpus is thought to have been authored by Hippocrates and perhaps his students and followers. The Hippocratic Oath defined good medical practice through an oath that was taken by physicians of the time. The original version, translated from Ionic Greek by Ludwig Edelstein, includes promises to keep patients "from harm and injustice," to not "give a deadly drug to anybody," to "not give to a woman an abortive remedy," and keep "what I may see or hear in the course of the treatment . . . to myself." The content of this version of the oath promising nonmaleficence (prevention of harm), disallowing euthanasia and abortion, and upholding patient privacy differ from the oaths that medical doctors take today, although there is some overlap.

In 1964, Louis Lasagna authored a modern version of the Hippocratic Oath, which is frequently used today. Most medical students take some form of the oath at graduation, although many critics charge that the oath-taking is a ritual without any binding force. In Lasagna's version there is no mention of nonmaleficence. Euthanasia and abortion are not singled out as medical practices, but Lasagna does note, "If it is given me to save a life, all thanks. But it may also be within my power to take a life; this awesome responsibility must be faced with great humbleness and awareness of my own frailty. Above all, I must not play at God." Without giving any specific directives, the oath here simply promises a level of reverence. As far as privacy, Lasagna specifically includes the oath, "I will respect the privacy of my patients, for their problems are not disclosed to me that the world may know." Overall, however, the updated Hippocratic Oath contains even less direct ethical guidance than the original.

The American Medical Association (AMA) demands that physician members adhere to a code of ethics. Among the nine principles it identifies, it includes respect for patient privacy and notes that physicians shall "regard responsibility to the patient as paramount." The AMA's Code of Medical Ethics allows physicians to perform abortions but claims that euthanasia is "fundamentally incompatible with the physician's role as healer." Opinions on a variety of other medical practices, including genetic testing and organ transplantation, are contained within the code of ethics. Nonetheless, the AMA only represents less than one-fifth of medical doctors. In addition, a 2011 survey by Jackson & Coker, a physician recruitment firm, found that only 11 percent of physicians polled agreed that the AMA's stance and actions represent their views, with 77 percent disagreeing. Thus, the AMA's Code of Medical Ethics is far from a consensus on the state of current accepted medical ethics.

Even where agreement can be found on broad ethical principles, just how they apply to various medical practices is far from resolved. The medical duty of nonmaleficence—the expectation that physicians do no harm—is the most well known of the values identified within the original Hippocratic Oath, but it is not the only one, as seen above. The phrase "first, do no harm" is not within the Hippocratic Oath, even though it is commonly attributed to it. The sentiment is there, however, and the duty to not harm patients is a fairly noncontroversial value of medical practice, in theory; but what this means in actual practice is not without controversy. Is helping a terminally ill patient who wants to end his or her life doing harm or not? Is administering chemotherapy with many harmful side effects a violation of the value of nonmaleficence or is it permissible in light of the goal of eradicating cancer? Even with the seemingly uncontroversial duty to do no harm, the questions that arise in the actual practice of medicine with regard to ethics are not easy to resolve and there are many competing viewpoints.

Ethical issues that arise in the context of medicine include the issue of access to necessary health care, which includes a variety of ethical dilemmas such as whether there is a right to basic preventative treatment as well as how access to lifesaving organ transplantation ought to be determined. With respect to particular medical treatments, ethical issues arise regarding regulation, especially in the rapidly developing fields of genetic and reproductive technologies. Finally, medical treatments related to the beginning and end of life are perennial lightning rods of controversy, with much public debate about issues such as euthanasia and abortion. These issues and many others are explored in *Current Controversies: Medical Ethics*, shedding light on the numerous ethical concerns that surround the field of medicine and the social controversy that accompanies these issues.

CHAPTER 1

What Ethics Should Guide the Health-Care System?

Overview: Americans' Approval of Healthcare Law Declines

Jeffrey M. Jones

Jeffrey M. Jones is a managing editor at the Gallup Poll.

Americans' views of the 2010 healthcare law have worsened in recent weeks, with 40% approving and 55% disapproving of it. For most of the past year, Americans have been divided on the law, usually tilting slightly toward disapproval. The now 15-percentage-point gap between disapproval and approval is the largest Gallup has measured in the past year.

The results are based on Gallup's annual Health and Healthcare poll, conducted Nov. 7–10.

Currently, 73% of Democrats, 39% of independents, and 8% of Republicans approve of the healthcare law. Approval is down at least marginally among all three groups since Gallup's last update in late October.

Since the government health insurance exchanges opened on Oct. 1, Americans' views of the healthcare law remained fairly steady even amid reports of widespread technical glitches with the websites.

More recently, President Barack Obama has had to respond to charges that he misled Americans when he repeatedly said those who liked their current insurance plans could keep them. Many insured Americans are now being dropped from their health plans, perhaps because the plans do not meet the minimum requirements for coverage mandated by the healthcare law. Obama has apologized for making those assurances and said he would explore options to help those affected.

The timing of this drop in approval of the law suggests it may be linked to the controversy over the millions of Americans losing their current health insurance coverage.

In fact, in an open-ended question probing Americans' reasons for approving or disapproving of the law, 11% of those who disapprove specifically mention losing their insurance. Another 7% say the president lied about details of the law.

Americans have been generally divided in their views of the [Affordable Care Act], both before and after its passage. Now, they are tilting more significantly toward disapproval.

These are not the most common reasons for disapproval, however. The leading complaint is a philosophical objection—government interference or forcing people to get healthcare—mentioned by 37% of those who disapprove. Twenty-one percent believe the law will increase costs and make healthcare less affordable. Eight percent specifically mention planning, design, or website problems; another 8% say the law is "not working."

The most common reason for approving of the law, mentioned by 23%, is the belief that it makes healthcare accessible to more people. Other common reasons for approval are the belief that everyone has a right to health insurance, that the law expands the number of insurance options available to Americans, will control costs, and covers people with pre-existing conditions.

Implications

Gallup has long found that Americans have been generally divided in their views of the healthcare law, both before and after its passage. Now, they are tilting more significantly toward disapproval.

That more negative evaluation may not have as much to do with the content of the law as the implementation of it, in particular how that squares with the president's earlier characterization of how the law would work.

Some Democratic members of Congress, as well as former President Bill Clinton, are urging the president to support legislation that would rewrite portions of the law to allow Americans to keep their insurance plan if they are being dropped from it, as a way to honor his pledge. At this point, it is not clear whether the president will seriously consider that, or attempt to adjust how the law is administered without rewriting pieces of it.

Additionally, many members of Congress from both parties are asking the administration to extend the deadline by a year for Americans to get health insurance before facing a fine, given the ongoing technical issues with the exchange websites, which are still being fixed. The White House recently extended the deadline by six weeks.

How the administration handles these challenges to the implementation of the law, plus any new ones that emerge in the coming months, could be critical in determining the trajectory of the "disapprove" line in Gallup's trend chart for the healthcare law.

Health Care Is a Right and Must Be Provided to All Americans

Bernie Sanders

Bernie Sanders is a US senator from Vermont; he is also registered as an independent member of Congress, though he caucuses with the Democratics.

I start my approach to healthcare from two very basic premises. First, healthcare must be recognized as a right, not a privilege. Every man, woman and child in our country should be able to access the healthcare they need regardless of their income. Second, we must create a national healthcare system that provides quality healthcare for all in the most cost-effective way possible.

Tragically, the United States is failing in both areas.

The US Healthcare System

It is unconscionable that in one of the most advanced nations in the world, there are nearly 50 million people who lack health insurance and millions more who have burdensome co-payments and deductibles. In fact, some 45,000 Americans die each year because they do not get to a doctor when they should. In terms of life expectancy, infant mortality and other health outcomes, the United States lags behind almost every other advanced country.

Despite this unimpressive record, the US spends almost twice as much per person on healthcare as any other nation. As a result of an incredibly wasteful, bureaucratic, profit-making and complicated system, the US spends 17% of its

Bernie Sanders, "A Single-Payer System, Like Medicare, Is the Cure for America's Ailing Healthcare," *Guardian* (UK), September 30, 2013. Copyright Guardian News & Media Ltd 2013. All rights reserved. Reproduced with permission.

gross domestic product—approximately $2.7tn [trillion] annually—on healthcare. While insurance companies, drug companies, private hospitals and medical equipment suppliers make huge profits, Americans spend more and get less for their healthcare dollars.

What should the US be doing to improve this abysmal situation?

President [Barack] Obama's Affordable Care Act is a start. It prevents insurance companies from denying patients coverage for pre-existing conditions, allows people up to age 26 to stay on their parents' insurance, sets minimum standards for what insurance must cover and helps lower-income Americans afford health insurance. When the marketplace exchanges open for enrollment on Tuesday [October 1, 2013], many Americans will find the premiums will be lower than the ones they're paying now. Others will find the coverage is much more comprehensive than their current plans.

A single-payer system would address one of the major deficiencies in the current system: the huge amount of money wasted on billing and administration.

Most importantly, another 20 million Americans will receive health insurance. This is a modest step forward. But if we are serious about providing quality care for all, much more needs to be done.

The Long-Term Solution

The only long-term solution to America's healthcare crisis is a single-payer national healthcare program.

The good news is that, in fact, a large-scale single-payer system already exists in the United States and its enrollees love it. It is called Medicare. Open to all Americans over 65 years of age, the program has been a resounding success since its introduction 48 years ago. Medicare should be expanded to cover all Americans.

Such a single-payer system would address one of the major deficiencies in the current system: the huge amount of money wasted on billing and administration. Hospitals and independent medical practices routinely employ more billing specialists than doctors—and that's not the end of it. Patients and their families spend an enormous amount of time and effort arguing with insurance companies and bill collectors over what is covered and what they owe. Drug companies and hospitals spend billions advertising their products and services.

Creating a simple system with one payer, covering all Americans, would result in an enormous reduction in administrative expenses. We would be spending our money on healthcare and disease prevention, not on paper-pushing and debt collection.

Further, a single-payer system will expand employment opportunities and lift a financial weight off of businesses encumbered by employee health expenses. Many Americans remain at their current jobs because of the decent health insurance provided by their employer. Without the worry of losing benefits, those Americans will be free to explore other, more productive opportunities as they desire. For business owners, lifting the burden of employee healthcare expenditures will free them to invest in growing their businesses.

The Need for a Single Federal Payer

Congressman Jim McDermott and I have introduced the American Health Security Act. Our bill will provide every American with healthcare coverage and services through a state-administered, single-payer program, including dental and mental health coverage and low-cost prescription drugs. It would require the government to develop national policies and guidelines, as well as minimum national criteria, while giving each state the flexibility to adapt the program as needed. It would also completely overhaul the health coverage system, creating a single federal payer of state-administered health plans.

The American people understand that our current healthcare system is not working. But the time is long overdue for them to understand that there is something fundamentally wrong when the US remains the only country in the industrialized world that does not guarantee healthcare to all its people.

Healthcare is a right and we must ensure provision of that right for Americans. A single-payer system will be good for the average American, good for businesses, good for workers and good for our overall economy.

It Is Immoral to Treat Health Care as a Right

Paul Hsieh

Paul Hsieh is a practicing diagnostic radiologist in Colorado and a founding member of Freedom and Individual Rights in Medicine (FIRM).

If someone in America needs medical care but cannot afford it, should he rely on charity or should others be forced to pay for it? President [Barack] Obama and his political allies say that Americans should be forced to pay for it. Forcing some Americans to pay medical bills for other Americans, says Obama, is a "moral imperative" and "the right thing to do."

No Right to Health Care

Throughout the health-care debate of 2010–11, Obama repeatedly referred to government-run health care as "a core ethical and moral obligation," arguing that, "No one should die because they cannot afford health care, and no one should go broke because they get sick." In speeches, he repeatedly cited the story of Natoma Canfield, an Ohio cancer patient without health insurance, as a justification for his health-care legislation. Many of Obama's supporters on the political left made similar moral claims. Vanderbilt University professor Bruce Barry wrote in the *New York Times* that, "Health insurance in a civilized society is a collective moral obligation." T.R. Reid, former foreign correspondent for the *Washington Post*, called universal health care a "moral imperative." Ezra Klein, another writer for the *Washington Post*, agreed that it is an "ethical obligation."

Paul Hsieh, "Health Care and the Separation of Charity and State," *Objective Standard*, vol. 6, no. 1, Spring 2011, pp. 17–19. Copyright © 2011 The Objective Standard. All rights reserved. Reproduced with permission.

But all such claims are wrong—*morally* wrong.

There is no "right" to health care. Rights are not entitlements to goods or services produced by others; rather, they are prerogatives to freedom of action, such as the right to free speech, the right to contract, or the right to use one's property. Any attempt to enforce a so-called "right" to health care necessarily violates the *actual* rights of those who are forced to provide or pay for that care.

Each individual must determine how best to allocate his resources in light of his own values. The government has no moral right to make such decisions for him.

If a patient needs a $50,000 operation but cannot afford it, he has the right to ask his friends, family, neighbors, or strangers for monetary assistance—and they have the right to offer it (or not). But the patient has no right to take people's money without their permission; to do so would be to violate their rights. His hardship, genuine as it may be, does not justify theft. Nor would the immoral nature of the act be changed by his taking $100 each from five hundred neighbors; that would merely spread the crime to a larger number of victims. Nor would the essence of the act change by his using the government as his agent to commit such theft on an even wider scale. The only moral way for this patient to receive the assistance he needs is for others to offer it *voluntarily*. Morally, he must rely on charity.

The Role of Charity

Fortunately for him, there is no shortage of people willing to offer charity, nor is there a shortage of reasons why one might self-interestedly wish to do so. Americans have always been magnificently generous in helping those in dire straits through no fault of their own. Recall the outpourings of aid that Americans have given to victims of natural and man-made disasters, such as hurricanes or the 9/11 attacks. As a physician, I have gladly provided free or discounted care to worthy patients more times than I can count, as has nearly every other doctor I know. Similarly, every year Americans donate hundreds of millions of dollars to health-related charitable organizations such as St. Jude's Children's Hospital, the Dana Farber Cancer Center, the American Cancer Society, and Susan G. Komen for the Cure. Fourteen of the fifty largest American charities are in the health-care sector, and many of these organizations help fund medical treatments for those who cannot afford them.

Americans donate to charitable causes for various rational, self-interested reasons. Some may want to fund treatments or research to help others fight an illness that affected a family member or friend. Others may take pleasure in knowing that they are helping unfortunate people live better lives than they would otherwise live. Whatever their reasons, many Americans give a lot of money to charity every year, and such giving is an affirmation of their values.

Conversely, some Americans choose *not* to donate to charities—whether because they have other priorities on which to spend their money, such as saving for their children's education or starting a business, or because they simply oppose the idea of giving to charity. People's priorities and policies are personal matters; each individual must determine how best to allocate his resources in light of his own values. The government has no moral right to make such decisions for him. The government's only proper function is to protect rights—including each individual's right to decide what to do with his hard-earned wealth.

The Separation of Charity and State

Morally, the government must maintain a "separation of charity and state," analogous to and for the same reason that it must maintain a "separation of church and state"—because individuals have a moral right to embrace and act on whatever ideas they regard as true and in their own interest, so long as they do not violate the same right of others.

Separation of church and state means that the government does not dictate whether or how men must practice religion; it leaves them free to engage in any religious practice they wish—or none at all. Similarly, separation of charity and state means the government does not dictate whether and to whom people should provide charity; it leaves them free to do so—or not—according to their own values, interests, and judgment. Just as a proper government does not force citizens to embrace Christianity or Judaism or atheism, so a proper government does not force citizens to work in a soup kitchen or donate to the Red Cross. And just as a proper government does not compel a man to support his neighbor's church, so a proper government does not compel a man to pay his neighbor's medical bills.

If Americans want to stop the government takeover of health care, we must stand up for individual rights and demand the separation of charity and state.

Public Health Insurance Programs Are Immoral and Unaffordable

D.W. MacKenzie

D.W. MacKenzie is an assistant professor of economics at Carroll College in Montana.

Recent difficulties with implementing the Affordable Care Act [ACA] have increased opposition to the program. A majority of Americans now oppose it. Problems with the healthcare.gov website are in all likelihood temporary. However, there are serious long-term problems, particularly considering long-term finance and labor-supply issues. Given the mounting difficulties with and growing concerns about the ACA, it is worthwhile to reconsider the main issues regarding this program.

The Cost of Federal Expenditures

The Congressional Budget Office (CBO) recently published a report examining some of these problems. It contains nothing new. Many commentators have discussed the projection of lower labor-force participation. Obamacare subsidies will allow lower-income Americans to work less. People do in fact work less if their costs are shared. The tendency of people to withhold work from collective undertakings is known among economists as a tragedy of the commons.

Reduced labor-force participation means both lower total tax revenue and higher spending on government benefits. The CBO's long-term forecasts report serious imbalances between tax revenues and federal spending. Federal deficits are pro-jected to remain high, but "manageable," for about a decade.

The costs of entitlements, along with regular budget items (defense and non-defense), are relevant to any discussion of the ACA's affordability. The retirement of the baby boomers, though, will result in steadily rising costs for older entitlement programs. Taxpayers are already legally responsible for a na-tional debt of $17 trillion (which will hit $20 trillion by the time [President Barack] Obama leaves office). Interest pay-ments on the national debt are low for the time being, but they won't stay that way forever. The Medicare trustees have admitted to a long-term deficit of $34 trillion, but indepen-dent estimates run much higher. Social Security has an un-funded liability of more than $12 trillion. These costs pile on top of the current regular budget of $3.5 trillion, not to men-tion projected growth in this budget. Taxpayers are also re-sponsible for the ACA's cost overruns. Section 1342 of the ACA makes taxpayers responsible for bailing out insurance companies if the need arises.

The U.S. government is heading toward bankruptcy su-perficially because politicians have failed to set rational budget priorities, and fundamentally because citizens ex-pect far too much of the public sector.

Taxpayers are *legally* obligated to finance all of the above-mentioned expenditures, debts, and unfunded liabilities. People who believe in individual liberty reject the idea that people are *morally* obliged to fund ever-rising federal expendi-tures. But the dispute over whether American taxpayers *should* fund projected federal spending is rendered academic by the fact that younger Americans will not be able to *afford* to pay for all of it. The commons created out of the New Deal and the Great Society is collapsing.

The Problem with Free Health Care

Economist Larry Kotlikoff estimates that average rates of taxation would have to rise 56 percent to cover projected increases in federal expenditures. Kotlikoff's estimate may be high, but even a lower figure would leave Americans in dire financial straits. Taxpayers simply will not be able to fund *all* projected increases in all current federal programs. Bond investors will not finance our rising national debt in unlimited amounts. The ACA's increased spending and lower labor-force participation, on top of these increases, makes national bankruptcy that much more likely.

National bankruptcy is not inevitable. The U.S. government is heading toward bankruptcy superficially because politicians have failed to set rational budget priorities, and fundamentally because citizens expect far too much of the public sector. The ACA was created out of concern that financial considerations bar access to healthcare to many people. And Americans do spend a large percentage of national income on healthcare.

The good news is that "we" have a substantial amount of leeway to save money on healthcare. Data on the overall effectiveness of public healthcare spending is clear, but not nearly as well known among voters. For example, The RAND Corporation conducted a health insurance experiment from 1974 to 1982, which showed that making healthcare "free," or available at no personal marginal cost, does lead people to buy more. Much of this extra healthcare is inappropriate or largely unneeded, however. When people pay for more of their healthcare out of pocket, they tend to waste less money. The RAND study concluded, "In general, the reduction in services induced by cost sharing had no adverse effect on participants' health." Many other studies cast doubt on the effectiveness of providing healthcare at no private cost. According to another study, "Medicare enrollees in higher-spending regions receive more care than those in lower-spending regions but do not have better health outcomes or satisfaction with care." Studies of people with health savings accounts (HSAs), as compared with people with plans like PPOs [preferred provider organizations], show HSA holders control premium inflation better than their PPO counterparts.

Passing costs onto someone else is, aside from being morally dubious, unworkable in the aggregate because we are each "someone else" to everyone else.

Having people pay deductibles or bear other out-of-pocket costs causes us to economize on healthcare. Health insurance pools risks and creates a type of commons, whether done privately or publicly. The private commons of insurance companies does, however, have limits. Private insurance companies deny some types of coverage, depending on how much insurance people contract for in the first place. In other words, private insurance is not an open commons—it specifies the extent to which each policy holder can draw out of the insurance pool.

Another Tragedy of the Commons

Public insurance programs lure people in by promising more benefits than private insurance plans offer. Yet public programs ultimately run into the basic problem of scarcity. The ACA pushes people out of very basic insurance plans into plans with higher levels of coverage but excessive coverage is a major source of high healthcare costs. Americans spend a sizable portion of GDP [gross domestic product] on health expenses (17.9 percent in 2011). The overconsumption of healthcare by overinsured Americans is both a major source of excessive costs and a cost that can be cut with little adverse effect.

The tendency of people to waste money in open-access healthcare financing is simply going to produce another tragedy of the commons. Too few young people have been signing up at Healthcare.gov because younger Americans are mostly smart enough to avoid paying into a commons. Americans are signing up mainly because they expect to draw subsidies out of this commons.

Problems with managing a commons in healthcare financing are serious. Once someone enters into a life-threatening medical condition they and their family will want every possible available step taken to save this person—provided that "someone else" pays. Passing costs onto someone else is, aside from being morally dubious, unworkable in the aggregate because we are each "someone else" to everyone else.

There are many costs associated with government intervention into the healthcare industry: administrative and regulatory compliance costs, elevated costs of litigation and court rulings, lobbying costs, costs of perverse incentives. The perversities associated with treating health as an open-access and politicized commons have, along with other, government spending programs, created an unsustainable fiscal situation. The unaffordability of the Affordable Care Act leaves us with two main options: Congress can repeal the ACA immediately through the legislative process, or we can all wait for the repeal process of national bankruptcy.

Public Health Insurance Programs Are Morally Required

Robert B. Reich

Robert B. Reich is the Chancellor's Professor of Public Policy at the University of California at Berkeley and senior fellow at the Blum Center for Developing Economies.

Having failed to defeat the Affordable Care Act in Congress, to beat it back in the last election, to repeal it despite more than eighty votes in the House, to stop it in the federal courts, to get enough votes in the Supreme Court to overrule it, and to gut it with outright extortion (closing the government and threatening to default on the nation's debts unless it was repealed), Republicans are now down to their last ploy.

The Republican Strategy

They are hell-bent on destroying the Affordable Care Act in Americans' minds.

A document circulating among House Republicans (reported by the *New York Times*) instructs them to repeat the following themes and stories continuously: "Because of Obamacare, I Lost My Insurance." "Obamacare Increases Health Care Costs." "The Exchanges May Not Be Secure, Putting Personal Information at Risk."

Every Republican in Washington has been programmed to use the word "disaster" whenever mentioning the Act, always refer to it as Obamacare, and demand its repeal.

Republican wordsmiths know they can count on Fox News and right-wing yell radio to amplify and intensify all of this in continuous loops of elaboration and outrage, repeated so often as to infect peoples' minds like purulent pustules.

The idea is to make the Act so detestable it becomes the fearsome centerpiece of the midterm elections of 2014—putting enough Democrats on the defensive they join in seeking its repeal or at least in amending it in ways that gut it (such as allowing insurers to sell whatever policies they want as long as they want, or delaying it further).

The Administration's Failures

Admittedly, the President provided Republicans ammunition by botching the Act's roll-out. Why wasn't HealthCare.gov up and running smoothly October 1? Partly because the Administration didn't anticipate that almost every Republican governor would refuse to set up a state exchange, thereby loading even more responsibility on an already over-worked and underfunded Department of Health and Human Services.

Ours has been the only healthcare system in the world designed to avoid sick people.

Why didn't Obama's advisors anticipate that some policies would be cancelled (after all, the Act sets higher standards than many policies offered) and therefore his "you can keep their old insurance" promise would become a target? Likely because they knew all policies were "grandfathered" for a year, didn't anticipate how many insurers would cancel right away, and understood that only 5 percent of policyholders received insurance independent of an employer anyway.

But there's really no good excuse. The White House should have anticipated the Republican attack machine.

Three Larger Truths

The real problem is now. The President and other Democrats aren't meeting the Republican barrage with three larger truths that show the pettiness of the attack:

The wreck of private insurance. Ours has been the only healthcare system in the world designed to avoid sick people. For-profit insurers have spent billions finding and marketing their policies to healthy people—young adults, people at low risk of expensive diseases, groups of professionals—while rejecting people with preexisting conditions, otherwise debilitated, or at high risk of heart disease, diabetes, and cancer. And have routinely dropped coverage of policy holders who become seriously sick or disabled. What else would you expect from corporations seeking to maximize profits?

But the social consequences have been devastating. We have ended up with the most expensive healthcare system in the world (finding and marketing to healthy people is expensive, corporate executives are expensive, profits adequate to satisfy shareholders are expensive), combined with the worst health outcomes of all rich countries—highest rates of infant mortality, shortest life spans, largest portions of populations never seeing a doctor and receiving no preventive care, most expensive uses of emergency rooms.

We could not and cannot continue with this travesty of a healthcare system.

The Affordable Care Act is a modest solution. It still relies on private insurers—merely setting minimum standards and "exchanges" where customers can compare policies, requiring insurers to take people with preexisting conditions and not abandon those who get seriously sick, and helping low-income people afford coverage.

A single-payer system would have been preferable. Most other rich countries do it this way. It could have been grafted on to Social Security and Medicare, paid for through payroll taxes, expanded to lower-income families through Medicaid. It would have been simple and efficient. (It's no coincidence that the Act's Medicaid expansion has been easy and rapid in states that chose to accept it.)

But Republicans were dead set against this. They wouldn't even abide a "public option" to buy into something resembling Medicare. In the end, they wouldn't even go along with the Affordable Care Act [ACA], which was based on Republican ideas in the first place. (From Richard Nixon's healthcare plan through the musings of the Heritage Foundation, Republicans for years urged that everything be kept in the hands of private insurers but the government set minimum standards, create state-based insurance exchanges, and require everyone to sign up).

It's only just that those with higher incomes bear some responsibility for maintaining the health of Americans who are less fortune.

The moral imperative. Even a clunky compromise like the ACA between a national system of health insurance and a for-profit insurance market depends, fundamentally, on a social compact in which those who are healthier and richer are willing to help those who are sicker and poorer. Such a social compact defines a society.

The other day I heard a young man say he'd rather pay a penalty than buy health insurance under the Act because, in his words, "why should I pay for the sick and the old?" The answer is he has a responsibility to do so, as a member the same society they inhabit.

The Act also depends on richer people paying higher taxes to finance health insurance for lower-income people. Starting this year, a healthcare surtax of 3.8 percent is applied to capital gains and dividend income of individuals earning more than $200,000 and a nine-tenths of 1 percent healthcare tax to wages over $200,000 or couples over $250,000. Together, the two taxes will raise an estimated $317.7 billion over 10 years, according to the Joint Committee on Taxation.

Here again, the justification is plain: We are becoming a vastly unequal society in which most of the economic gains are going to the top. It's only just that those with higher incomes bear some responsibility for maintaining the health of Americans who are less fortune.

The Moral Argument

This is a profoundly moral argument about who we are and what we owe each other as Americans. But Democrats have failed to make it, perhaps because they're reluctant to admit that the Act involves any redistribution at all.

Redistribution has become so unfashionable it's easier to say everyone comes out ahead. And everyone does come out ahead in the long term: Even the best-off will gain from a healthier and more productive workforce, and will save money from preventive care that reduces the number of destitute people using emergency rooms when they become seriously ill.

But there would be no reason to reform and extend health insurance to begin with if we did not have moral obligations to one another as members of the same society.

The initial problems with the website and the President's ill-advised remark about everyone being able to keep their old policies are real. But they're trifling compared to the wreckage of the current system, the modest but important step toward reform embodied in the Act, and the moral imperative at the core of the Act and of our society.

The Republicans have created a tempest out of trivialities. It is incumbent on Democrats—from the President on down—to show Americans the larger picture, and do so again and again.

Conscience Exemptions for Individuals and Businesses Are Needed

Edmund F. Haislmaier

Edmund F. Haislmaier is a senior research fellow in health policy studies at The Heritage Foundation.

Discussions of the ethics of health care financing typically focus on issues of equity and social justice. Yet such discussions are more often about means than ends. Contrary to the impression given by occasionally heated political rhetoric, there, in fact, exists a broad consensus across the political spectrum that modern societies have an obligation to ensure that all of their members have access to needed medical care.

The Debates

Of course, there are still disagreements over what should be considered necessary or appropriate care, or where to draw the line between personal and collective financial responsibilities, but those are mainly disputes at the margins.

Somewhat more consequential are the debates over how the system should be structured. They involve not only disagreements over the proper roles of the government and the private sector, but also practical considerations with respect to the efficacy of different approaches for organizing the financing and delivery of medical care.

The same can also be found in other social policy areas, such as education. For instance, the existence of broad societal support for the proposition that all children should be educated to a minimum level, does not, in and of itself, resolve questions over how best to achieve that end, the appropriate level of resources to devote to the effort, how the system should be structured, or the proper roles of the various participants.

Rather, in health care financing, the truly contentious issues today are those that center on the morality of specific therapies or actions. Indeed, recent scientific advances are spawning new ethical issues in medicine—and by extension, in health care financing as well. To the issues that have long been present, such as abortion, euthanasia, and assisted suicide, must now be added others, such as artificial contraception, assisted reproduction, sex-change treatments, genetic therapies, therapeutic cloning, and potential therapies derived from embryonic stem cells.

Employer-Sponsored Health Insurance

While these issues typically attract attention in the context of debates over the use of public funds, such as the issue of paying for abortion in public programs, they also exist, though less visibly, in private health care financing. That is particularly the case in the United States, where half of all medical care is still privately financed, mainly through employer-provided health insurance.

Most workers probably do not know if their employer's health plan uses their money to pay for items or services that they consider immoral.

Private, employer-sponsored health insurance has been the dominant form of medical coverage in the United States for over half a century. Even though the share of the population covered by employer health plans has declined from its peak in the 1970s, 58.4 percent of the non-elderly U.S. population is still covered by employment-based health insurance. This arrangement is the product of social policies since the 1940s that have favored it, mainly by treating employer-provided health benefits as tax-free income to workers. In the intervening years, government also imposed regulations on these arrangements, but until now those regulations were almost exclusively limited to addressing the contractual and financial aspects of private coverage.

However, this coverage arrangement presents its own set of ethical considerations, and while the latest federal health care legislation has pushed those issues to the forefront, they have long been present in the system in latent form.

Employer-sponsored health insurance is a form of compensation paid by an employer to its workers. As such, the ethics of how those funds are spent is of consequence to both the employer and the workers. Moral obligations attach not only to the employer's decisions with respect to selecting or designing the plan, but also to the employee's participation in the plan, since such plans are collective arrangements funded with monies that would otherwise be part of the worker's cash wages.

Yet, most workers probably do not know if their employer's health plan uses their money to pay for items or services that they consider immoral. They might be surprised to learn, for example, that a 2003 health care coverage survey found that 46 percent of workers with employer-sponsored health insurance were covered by plans that paid for abortion services. Indeed, there have been instances in which even conscientious employers, including some Catholic institutions, discovered that they had been, unintentionally, providing their workers with health plans that include coverage for morally objectionable items or procedures.

Changing Social Norms Responsible

These situations occur because changing social norms and developments in medical science have steadily altered what is considered "standard" or "typical" in employer health plan coverage. Unless an employer is diligent in excluding morally objectionable services from its health plan coverage, one or more of those services are increasingly likely to be in the plan by default.

[The Affordable Care Act] expands federal government regulation of private health care coverage in a number of significant ways.

To this equation has now been added another dimension by the most recent federal health care legislation, the Patient Protection and Affordable Care Act (PPACA) of 2010. While that legislation does expand existing public programs somewhat, its more consequential feature is that it takes the novel approach of attempting to achieve social policy objectives by compelling individuals to engage in government-specified transactions with other private parties. In effect, rather than increasing taxation to the level necessary to achieve its objectives through public programs, Congress instead decided to commandeer existing private resources to achieve those objectives through closely regulated private arrangements.

That this approach is novel in terms of secular law can be seen from the challenges to the constitutionality of the law's requirement that individuals purchase health insurance. However, it is also novel with respect to the ethics of health care financing, in that it shifts the locus of authority over private medical treatment and private financing decisions, including those that entail ethical or moral considerations, from employers and individuals to government.

A Shift in Authority

The legislation expands federal government regulation of private health care coverage in a number of significant ways, three of which embody this significant shift in authority:

First, it grants the U.S. Department of Health and Human Services (HHS) sweeping new powers to impose a wide range of benefit requirements on policies sold by health insurers and, in some cases, on employer-sponsored health plans as well.

Second, for the first time, it requires employers with 50 or more workers to provide their employees with health insurance coverage that the federal government deems to be adequate and affordable, or pay annual fines for failing to comply.

Third, and also for the first time, it requires individuals to obtain the minimum health insurance coverage specified by the government, or pay annual fines for failing to comply.

The Public Accommodation Rationale

Underlying these measures is a corresponding shift in the rationale for government regulation that has profound implications for the ethics of private health care financing.

In October 2010, a major medical journal published a paper by a leading supporter [George Washington University professor Sara Rosenbaum] of the legislation arguing for the constitutionality of its requirement on individuals to obtain health insurance. Setting aside the merits of the legal reasoning, it is the author's exposition of the law's underlying philosophical rationale that is most clarifying for our purposes. The principal justification offered for the requirement on individuals to obtain health insurance is that it is part of "a broader regulatory scheme" embodied in the new law:

> First, and perhaps most fundamentally, in a remarkable shift whose precedent lies in the watershed Civil Rights Act of 1964, the [PPACA] transforms health insurance into a public accommodation. . . . This basic reconceptualization of health insurance as a good whose availability is a matter of national public interest essentially frames health insurance the way the Civil Rights Act framed other business interests.

It is under this "public accommodation" rationale that the government now asserts the power to: (1) require employers to fund and manage health plans for their workers; (2) compel individuals to purchase health coverage; and (3) determine the scope and benefits of the coverage that must be provided and purchased. Because some of those decisions will involve ethical or moral considerations, the government is also implicitly asserting the supremacy of its own moral judgments over those of the employers and workers whose resources pay for the medical care in question.

Starting in 2014, insurers will be required to include the essential health benefits in all individual and small-group policies.

The Ongoing Conflict

The first conflict to arise out of the government's exercise of these new powers centers on the requirement that employers and individuals pay for and facilitate contraception, sterilization, and abortion-inducing drugs. However, it is not hard to envision more such conflicts arising in the future, should this new arrogation of power by the government be permitted to stand. That is because the legislation's two separate benefit-setting provisions are drafted as broad grants of discretionary authority to the executive branch.

First, Congress empowered HHS to define and "periodically update," a package of "essential health benefits" within at least 10 broad categories. Starting in 2014, insurers will be required to include the essential health benefits in all individual and small-group policies.

Second, the law requires both insurers and employers, including those that "self-insure," to cover specified "preventive services" with no enrollee cost-sharing. The requirement that employers and insurers provide coverage for contraception (including abortion-inducing drugs) and sterilization, is a subset of this second set of benefit mandates.

With these provisions now in federal law, there will likely be interest group pressure to expand the list of mandated benefits, and some of those proposed additions are likely to also be morally objectionable. Indeed, that has been the experience with benefit mandates imposed by state governments on insurers, though employers can avoid state government mandates by not purchasing coverage from an insurance company and instead designing and funding their own "self-insured" plans. However, that solution will not work for the subset of new federal benefit mandates that are imposed not only on insurers but also directly on employers.

Thus, both employers and individuals attempting to act in accordance with Catholic moral teaching are placed in an unsatisfactory position.

Pursuing court challenges to the infringement on rights of conscience posed by morally objectionable government benefit mandates is important, but it . . . will not produce a definitive resolution.

The Unsatisfactory Solutions

One option for a Catholic or other conscientious employer, would be to simply discontinue the employee health plan and convert plan contributions back into cash wages paid to the workers. However, under the new law, if the employer has 50 or more workers, it would then be fined $2,000 each year, per worker, for not providing the required coverage. Furthermore, its workers would also be fined if they did not, then, obtain the required coverage on their own. Yet, all of the alternative plans available to them in either the individual insurance market, or through the employer of another worker in the family, would be required to include the morally objectionable items or services. Thus, this option is not a satisfactory solution for either the employer or the employees.

Another option would be for employers who are conscientious objectors to redesign their employee health benefit plans in ways that:

1. exclude coverage of morally objectionable items and services, and thus do not violate their consciences;

2. avoid exposing their organizations to the ruinous fines imposed on non-compliant plans, yet; and

3. still enable them to offer their workers employer-sponsored health benefits on a pre-tax basis.

I have been working with others who also have expertise in this area to develop a template for such benefit plan redesigns that Catholic and other objecting employers could use. However, under this approach, the employer would still be fined the same as if he provided no coverage, and his employees would also be fined if they did not otherwise obtain the required coverage. Thus, while creatively redesigning employer plans could significantly reduce the risks and costs associated with non-compliance—relieving some of the pressure on employers as they await the eventual disposition of their legal challenges—this option also does not resolve the underlying conflict.

Of course, pursuing court challenges to the infringement on rights of conscience posed by morally objectionable government benefit mandates is important, but it, too, will not produce a definitive resolution. Even if the plaintiffs challenging the imposition of the contraceptive coverage mandate eventually prevail in court, the government would still retain the power to later impose one or more other morally objectionable coverage requirements. Each future infringement would have to be litigated all over again.

A Conscience Exemption

A more definitive solution would be to add a "conscience exemption" to the law. Yet, to be truly satisfactory, a conscience exemption would need to meet at least the following four tests:

1. It would need to be explicit and unambiguous.

2. It would need to broadly protect conscience rights with respect to decisions not only involving existing items, services, and treatments, but future ones as well.

3. It would need to be available, on equal terms and as a matter of right, to any individual or entity, and could not be otherwise conditional or dependent on government deciding the validity of conscience claims.

4. It would need to be functionally meaningful by also permitting health insurers to offer plans that exclude from coverage specific items or services if their customers have moral objections to funding or facilitating those items or services.

The Church's teaching on the inherent dignity and worth of every human life should be the guiding principle for ... constructing a comprehensive and equitable system for financing and delivering medical care.

Yet, the very need for such an amendment indicates that the basic structure of the underlying law is seriously flawed. A law crafted such that it can be applied justly only if significant exceptions are permitted, is inherently defective in either its basic premise or its basic design, or both. In such circumstances, it is best for lawmakers to simply repeal the defective law. Assuming that the original objectives are legitimate, lawmakers may then adopt other, less problematic, means to achieving the same ends.

It is possible to ensure that all members of society have access to needed medical care, accompanied by just and equitable financing arrangements, without resorting to laws that infringe on freedom of religion and conscience.

The Role of Church Guidance

While designing such an alternative approach involves practical considerations that are outside the scope of the Church's moral and teaching authority, it is possible, and indeed helpful, for the Church to offer additional guidance derived from other principles beyond those of equity and social justice.

To return to the earlier analogy, if there are multiple ways to structure a system of universal primary education, then, in order to assess the relative merits of those competing approaches, one must look for guidance to some other principle beyond that of social justice. In the case of education, that principle should be the Church's teaching that parents are the ones who have the primary responsibility and authority in educating their children. Judged in light of that principle, an educational system that operates with more deference to the rights and authority of parents would be preferable to one that gives less deference.

In the same fashion, the Church's teaching on the inherent dignity and worth of every human life should be the guiding principle for assessing the relative merits of differing approaches to constructing a comprehensive and equitable system for financing and delivering medical care.

The Primacy of Patients

The system will function best and most effectively if it is structured such that patients and consumers—not governments or employers—are empowered to be the ultimate decision-makers. It is possible to construct a comprehensive, just, and equitable health care system without subordinating the needs and authority of patients to those of government, employers, insurers, or medical providers. My colleagues and I have spent years working on the details of how that can, in fact, be accomplished.

We also argued several years ago that greater patient and consumer control over health care financing was also the best way to ultimately, and more satisfactorily, address the growing number of issues in biomedical ethics.

While the Church rightly does not pronounce on prudential matters that do not have direct moral implications, it does point to the relevant, basic principles that should guide our assessments of the total effects of social structures and public policies.

To adapt a formulation sometimes used in other contexts, I submit that, just as the totality of Catholic teaching should lead us in education policy to a preferential option for solutions built around the primacy of parents, so, too, it should lead us in health care policy to a preferential option for solutions built around the primacy of patients. That primacy is not just a primacy of their needs, or even a primacy of their authority. It is also a primacy of their conscience.

Religious Freedom Should Not Allow Employers to Deny Medical Care

Marci A. Hamilton

Marci A. Hamilton is the Paul R. Verkuil Chair in Public Law at the Benjamin N. Cardozo School of Law, Yeshiva University, and the author of God vs. the Gavel: The Perils of Extreme Religious Liberty.

So the Supreme Court came down with its historic interpretation of the Religious Freedom Restoration Act (RFRA) [June 30, 2014] today in the decisions of *Burwell v. Hobby Lobby* and *Conestoga Wood v. Burwell*. In a nutshell, the Court held that religious owners of closely held corporations can use their religious beliefs to determine what medical treatments will be covered by company health plans—without reference to the religious beliefs of the employees. Specifically, female employees can be denied coverage for contraception—either some or all (depending on the particular religious beliefs of the employer)—because the employer doesn't believe anyone should use it, and does not want to have to pay into a plan where women might make a choice to use it, say, after they were raped.

It is simply a fact that five male Catholic Supreme Court Justices have now transformed what is already a bad law into a truly dangerous one, all for the apparent purpose of undermining women's access to contraception. Whatever the legal reasoning, the optics are very bad on this one, and whether intentionally or not, they stoke the perception that the Justices are in league with the Catholic bishops in the latter's attempt to turn the clock back on not just *Roe v. Wade* [protecting the right to abortion] but also *Griswold v. Connecticut* [protecting the right to contraception]. . . .

The First Amendment and RFRA

The majority decision, written by Justice Samuel Alito, along with Justice Anthony Kennedy's concurrence, are peppered with attempts to limit the decision to contraception and women, which is ugly enough, but these attempts to limit its actual impact are unpersuasive if one understands the law. This is, in fact, a sly opinion that not only delivers free exercise rights to for-profit corporations without meaningful consideration of the impact on their employees but also renders an interpretation of key elements of RFRA that render it a mightier sword than it ever was. RFRA's ugly underbelly and its pretense to reflect the First Amendment are now in full view.

The United States' successful, long-honored balance between religious freedom and the rule of law was displaced by RFRA, which invites religious adherents to demand a right not only to believe and practice but also to impose their beliefs on others.

Yet, the Court did us all a favor by explicitly stating that RFRA does not restore the First Amendment's doctrine, but is more extreme. Under RFRA, a believer must prove that a law imposes a "substantial burden" on religious conduct. If the believer succeeds, then the burden shifts to the government to prove that the law serves a "compelling interest" through "the least restrictive means." . . .

This was never the Supreme Court's First Amendment standard, which means that the word "Restoration" in the title of the Act is actually a misrepresentation. More accurate would be: Religious Freedom Power Grab Act, or RFPGA.

In a refreshing moment in the religious culture wars, the Supreme Court today did make explicit that this was never its standard and that RFRA goes well beyond its First Amendment cases, in footnote 3 and the accompanying text. Thank you, to the Court, for at least that truthfulness. We can now rid this debate of those who keep trying to dress this RFRA wolf in sheep's clothing with statements like, RFRA merely codified what has been "the law for 50 years." No, this has been the law for a few years, and it has been a bad law that is driving our culture to unprecedented discord and Balkanization. The United States' successful, long-honored balance between religious freedom and the rule of law was displaced by RFRA, which invites religious adherents to demand a right not only to believe and practice but also to impose their beliefs on others.

The Meaning of Substantial Burden

Before today, "substantial burden" placed a meaningful burden of proof on a believer. It was a threshold requirement that kept some sanity in the free exercise universe. Unfortunately, in this decision, the majority finds a "substantial" burden where the burden is at most indirect, and decidedly attenuated. The Court characterizes it, saying the company owners must "arrange for such coverage," which requires them to "engage in conduct that seriously violates their religious beliefs." In other words, the mere arranging for coverage—which they themselves will never use, and will never know if their employees use it (due to the federal health privacy laws)— imposes a burden. This is not just a small burden but a substantial one. This makes absolutely no sense unless one counts psychic, speculative burdens on liberty as substantial. Before today, such arguments at the Supreme Court were nonstarters.

But the Court goes on to say that if the companies do not comply, there are hefty fines and taxes. Those apparently are truly substantial from the Court's view (though Hobby Lobby has gross profits of billions of dollars per year, a fact the Court fails to acknowledge). The Court refuses to consider the amici's [supporters'] arguments that the numbers were not what the believers say they are, and faults the government for not making those "intensely empirical" arguments itself. In short, it defers to the beleivers' math and rejects everyone else's. So RFRA renders a win on "substantial burden" because the government did not offer enough empirical evidence to justify its policy choice.

Apparently, if the burden on the believer is financial, the answer is for the government (aka taxpayers) to alleviate that burden by paying instead.

If it sounds like this element of RFRA is being employed to make the Supreme Court a super-legislature, it is. That is one of the reasons RFRA violates the separation of powers, as I explain in my amicus brief, which is an issue the Court does not address.

The Least Restrictive Test

The least restrictive means test was never adopted by the Supreme Court in its free exercise cases. In fact, a church attempted to persuade the Court that was the standard, but failed abysmally five months before RFRA was passed in *Church of Lukumi Babalu Ave v. City of Hialeah*. Still, it is the test in RFRA, and the Court here, acknowledging that it is "exceptionally demanding," took it in a new, extreme direction.

The least restrictive means is the means that will least burden this believer and still serve the government's compelling interest. So Hobby Lobby and Conestoga Wood say that they are burdened by having to subsidize contraception for their female employees. What would be less restrictive? Well, in a world of common sense, that answer would be that it's not even a burden anyway, as I discuss above, but let's pretend with the Court that the law does impose a substantial burden. What would lessen it?

Aha!! Let someone else pay for it! There are three options, according to the Court. First, the government. The Court actually says that the government has not proven that the cost of providing contraception *itself* would not be feasible. The government, rightly in my view, responded in briefing to such an argument with "RFRA cannot be used to require creation of entirely new programs." Not so, says the Court. The Affordable Care Act costs $1.3 trillion, so what's a little additional cost for paying for women's contraception? Apparently, if the burden on the believer is financial, the answer is for the government (aka taxpayers) to alleviate that burden by paying instead.

Second, the employees. Because the government would have to enact legislation to realize the first option, and that is not guaranteed with a Republican House, another option is that women will get stuck paying for their own contraception. The quirk here is that if their religious beliefs require responsible family planning or emergency contraception following a rape, that does not matter. Only the employers' beliefs matter.

The tide in favor of RFRA has turned, though, with the progressive groups that supported the religious groups to obtain RFRA's passage in the first instance awake to RFRA's inherent dangers.

Third, the insurance companies. The Court points to the accommodation already in place for nonprofit religious organizations: They can "self-certify that [they] oppose[] providing coverage for particular contraceptive services," leaving a third-party insurance company to pay for the coverage. In other words, because the government had offered an accommodation to nonprofit religious entities, that same accommodation should be offered to for-profit entities. Yes, that is less restrictive on the for-profit corporations, no doubt.

In short, let *anyone* pay but Hobby Lobby and Conestoga Wood, whose employees likely don't even share the same beliefs on contraception. So much for a net win for religious liberty. It's a win for religious oppression, though.

The Future of RFRA

This decision reveals RFRA in all its subversive and ugly glory. It empowers the powerful at the expense of the vulnerable. It invites believers to impose their beliefs on others. It is a weapon.

Justice [Ruth Bader] Ginsburg is correct that the majority provided a "decision of startling breadth," possibly applying to "employers with religiously grounded objections to blood transfusions (Jehovah's Witnesses); antidepressants (Scientologists); medications derived from pigs, including anesthesia, intravenous fluids, and pills coated with gelatin (certain Muslims, Jews, and Hindus); and vaccinations (Christian Scientists, among others)."

The tide in favor of RFRA has turned, though, with the progressive groups that supported the religious groups to obtain RFRA's passage in the first instance awake to RFRA's inherent dangers. It is heartening to see the likes of the ACLU and Americans United for Separation of Church and State and Planned Parenthood taking a stand against extreme religious liberty. And they are now joined by gay rights groups and children's advocates who deeply understand the harm that can be done in the name of religion.

RFRA should be repealed before we further test the limits of the insatiable demands for religious liberty at the expense of too many others.

CHAPTER 2

What Ethics Should Guide Organ Transplants?

Overview: Fairness in Dispensing Donated Organs

Catherine Hollander

Catherine Hollander covers economics as a correspondent for the National Journal.

For the past 60 years, doctors have been able to take an organ from one person and transplant it into another. The practice got off to a bumpy start, sometimes extending lives for only days, rather than the years we now expect. But it was soon prey to its own success: By the 1980s, there clearly weren't enough organs to go around. Hospitals needed ways to decide who would live and who would die, and early criteria included a tally of who had been in the hospital the longest and notions of "social worth"—income, education, community standing.

The Transformation in Transplant Ethics

The case of Sarah Murnaghan shows how far we've come since then. The 10-year-old has cystic fibrosis, and she wasn't likely to survive without a new set of lungs. Transplant ethics now aim to maximize utility—assessors try to calculate the "transplant benefit measure," or additional days of life a recipient could have—rather than to practice social Darwinism. But only for adults. While Murnaghan had her whole life ahead of her, the rules also aim to reduce the risk of wasted organs, so she wasn't eligible to receive an adult lung that might not take. When her family, state politicians, and a judge intervened on her behalf, they became part of the long struggle to find a scientific sweet spot between urgency and outcomes—and highlighted how far we've come since the former ruled the day.

The transformation began slowly, as medical developments pushed providers to make decisions based on science rather than social status. For now, there's no legislation on the books about how to calculate the number of years someone is expected to live beyond a transplant. The National Organ Transplant Act of 1984 made it illegal to buy and sell organs (a fear born of the widening supply-and-demand gap) and set up the Organ Procurement and Transplantation Network [OPTN], run by transplant surgeons and others who decide the allocation policies for each body part. This group, which manages some 120,000 patients on U.S. organ-transplant waiting lists, is overseen by the Health and Human Services Department [HHS].

The notion that we would distribute organs according to who could mount a PR campaign, get the attention of a congressman and a judge, is not the way to distribute organs.

The OPTN says, for example, that potential lung recipients are scored according to 13 criteria, including pulmonary artery pressure, body-mass index, and the distance a person can walk in six minutes. Children have a separate list, because the OPTN says it lacks sufficient data on these transplants, such as procedures to pare adult lungs for children's chests. Kids' place in the queue is governed more by the old-fashioned rules: How urgent is their need? So when Murnaghan's parents begged to have their daughter moved from the under-12 list to the adult list, which has access to a much larger pool of lungs, their appeal went all the way to HHS Secretary Kathleen Sebelius.

Last month [June 2013], Sebelius declined to intervene. "The worst of all worlds, in my mind, is to have some individual pick and choose who lives and who dies," she said at a House hearing. "You want a process where it's guided by medical science and medical experts." The Murnaghans sued. Sen. Pat Toomey and Rep. Pat Meehan, both Pennsylvania Republicans, publicly urged Sebelius to exempt Murnaghan from the OPTN policy. In June, the federal District Court in eastern Pennsylvania ruled that Sebelius could not keep Murnaghan and another 11-year-old with cystic fibrosis, Javier Acosta, off the adult waiting list.

The Terrible Reality of Organ Transplantation

But could the young bodies assimilate the grown-up organs? Arthur Caplan, director of the division of medical ethics at New York University's Langone Medical Center, estimates that in the 10 years since the lung-paring procedure was developed, maybe 20 adult-to-child transplants have been done. The OPTN cites the absence of data as the reason for its separate-list policy, but the court allowed Murnaghan onto the adult list, saying it wasn't clear a transplant *wouldn't* work. "This was an area that was more open, if you will, to debate or political arm-twisting, because it's not as well-established a procedure," Caplan says. "But, in general, the notion that we would distribute organs according to who could mount a PR [public relations] campaign, get the attention of a congressman and a judge, is not the way to distribute organs."

This isn't the first time political forces have advocated on behalf of patients. In 1983, an 11-month-old Texas girl, Ashley Bailey, was dying of biliary atresia, a disease that causes liver failure. President [Ronald] Reagan used his weekly radio address to aid the search, offering an Air Force jet to transport the liver if necessary. (More broadly, he urged Americans to become organ donors.) Bailey died, because organs are rarely available for babies. But Reagan's intentions notwithstanding, ethicists say it's best for politicians not to interfere: It gives some recipients an unfair advantage—one not earned on the outcome-focused standard. The science-based approach is supposed to give everyone a fair shot.

Of course, as cases like Sarah Murnaghan's illustrate, it's not always clear what constitutes a "fair shot." She received her transplant one week after the court ruling. But her political advocates didn't know the medical risks, and they effectively pushed organ allocation, in her case, back to a time before proven science dominated the calculus. It also revealed just how far the science has progressed—that we, as patients and consumers, now expect quality outcomes. Murnaghan's initial lung transplant failed right away. She received a second transplant later in the month and now appears to be making small steps toward recovery. "This is an incredibly agonizing situation, where someone lives and someone dies," Sebelius told lawmakers last month. The terrible reality of organ transplantation today is that there just aren't enough organs.

Presumed Consent Is the Most Ethical and Effective Organ Donation System

Stu Strumwasser

Stu Strumwasser is a writer, business executive, and entrepreneur.

Eighteen Americans will die today while waiting for a kidney. For many of them, that didn't need to be the case.

This sad fact gets far less attention than it deserves. Perhaps more remarkable than the sheer number of deaths is the fact that it is a political failure—not a medical one. We can chalk it up as one of the many consequences of a gridlocked legislature. The issue is not sensational enough to generate discussion on the Sunday morning talk shows and instead falls into the much larger bucket of topics that legislators simply don't care enough about, or that a broken government doesn't have the time to address. However, it may soon grow into an unavoidable problem.

The Organ Shortage

Consider a few alarming statistics: The waiting lists for organ recipient candidates broke 100,000 names in 2008. As of March 21, 2014, it now exceeds 121,000. Approximately 80 percent of those on the lists are waiting for kidneys (a redundant organ of which humans have two, but only need one to live normal and healthy lives, provided that donors receive proper postsurgical care). Another 15 percent or so of those on the waiting list are waiting for livers. While humans only have one

Stu Strumwasser, "The Tragedy of American Organ Donations: So Many More People Could Be Saved," *Salon*, March 23, 2014. This article first appeared in Salon.com, at http://www.Salon.com. An online version remains in the Salon archives. All rights reserved. Reprinted with permission.

liver, the organ has two major blood supplies and, unlike the cells that constitute many other organs, liver cells re-grow. It is therefore possible for living donors to gift one third of a healthy and functioning liver to a recipient and, in otherwise-healthy patients, have both the donor and recipient eventually re-grow an entire, fully-functioning liver.

Currently, the average wait for a kidney is around seven years. While patients in the end stages of renal disease (ESRD) wait for a kidney, they must undergo dialysis three times a week in uncomfortable four-hour sessions, for years, while their overall health deteriorates. The later they receive a transplant, the less likely they are to survive. In addition, there are approximately 300,000 other Americans presently on dialysis who are not even counted on the waiting lists for kidneys as they are either too old or too sick to qualify as recipients, or have simply not yet been added. Each day their ranks grow.

Incredibly, in the case of the organ shortage, the problem is not the expense of a potential solution; there are actually billions of dollars that could be saved annually with the introduction of corrective legislation.

Is there simply nothing we can do? No. The tragic aspect of this particular shortage is that there are plenty of organs and there *are* things we can do. Yet, this year we will lose more than 7,000 Americans, many of whom will be buried unnecessarily.

The chain of events that causes the organ shortage begins with overeating and poor nutrition, which have attracted a great deal of attention in recent years—while awareness of the resulting shortage of kidneys has not yet made the agenda of the mainstream media. As the epidemic of obesity continues to grow in the U.S., the incidence of diabetes also increases, resulting in an expanding number of patients with end-stage renal disease—many of whom land on waiting lists for kidneys.

Incredibly, in the case of the organ shortage, the problem is not the expense of a potential solution; there are actually billions of dollars that could be *saved* annually with the introduction of corrective legislation. From a financial perspective, here's how it breaks down: As of 2008, dialysis typically cost between $30,000 and $80,000 per patient per year. Most of that expense ultimately falls on Medicare, meaning it is funded by taxpayers. According to Medpac's *Report To The Congress: Medicare Payment Policy*, March 2012,

> In 2010, more than 355,000 ESRD beneficiaries on dialysis were covered under fee-for-service (FFS) Medicare and received dialysis from about 5,500 ESRD facilities. In that year, Medicare expenditures for outpatient dialysis services, including separately billable drugs administered during dialysis, were $9.5 billion.

Every year there are more patients waiting for a longer time, meaning that the cost of maintaining those dialysis patients grows with each passing year, and each passing session of Congress. It is quickly becoming a financial epidemic—in addition to a medical one—and all of it could be effectively addressed by creating better access to more kidneys. If ever there was an issue Republicans and Democrats should agree upon, it's an opportunity to save the lives of thousands of Americans, help thousands more and save money while doing it.

A Three-Step Solution to the Organ Shortage

In addition to long-term educational programs to improve nutrition and reduce obesity for Americans, a viable near-term solution to the organ shortage must be three-pronged:

Step 1: Better education and enforcement of legally-binding donor commitments.

The first part of the solution depends on the education of hospital staffers and the families of recently deceased or brain-dead loved ones—as well as enforcement of laws that make registration as an organ donor legally binding. (Many states have such laws, but enforcement remains uneven.) More effective awareness and educational campaigns are needed to dispel common myths, such as the misconception that "brain-dead" patients can recover, when they actually can't, or that doctors will try less to save someone who is a registered organ donor.

While there is effectively no reason that a hospital must *accept an organ donation from a decedent over the objections of her family ... there are many reasons that doing so could pose risks.*

Even when a potential organ donor has registered on his driver's license, signed up for the official registry and gone so far as to explain his wishes to his family prior to death, there is no guarantee that his wishes will be honored at the critical time. Even in states where registration is "legally binding," a donor's wishes are often quickly set aside by hospital personnel when confronted with objections by distraught family members at the worst of times. (Just imagine if family members could simply ignore their loved one's wishes regarding his or her finances after death. Shouldn't the fate of a person's body be the individual's choice just as much as the dispersal of his money?)

The problem is, while there is effectively no reason that a hospital *must* accept an organ donation from a decedent over the objections of her family—because of the aforementioned lax enforcement—there are many reasons that doing so could pose risks, including but not limited to lawsuits, bad press and an overall reduction in additional donors thereafter.

An article in the *Southern Medical Journal* in 2004—titled, "When Is an Organ Donor Not an Organ Donor?"—pointed out the following:

> The Uniform Anatomical Gift Act (UAGA) grants any competent adult the legal right to designate whether he or she wishes to donate his or her organs for transplantation after death.... [T]he individual, not the family, should determine the postmortem disposition of the individual's body. The patient's wishes while living should extend after death, regardless of relatives' objections.

The article goes on to explain that "Family refusals to donate (even when the patient's wish to be an organ donor was clearly elaborated before death) constitute a major source of lost donations. Each year in the United States, relatives refuse donation of and bury at least 5,000 organs that are medically suitable for transplantation."

Simply put, a commitment is a commitment. There should not be a choice.

Step 2: Implement a modern opt-out system of presumed consent.

In the U.S., we utilize an "opt in" system for organ donation. Unless you actively agree to be a donor, your organs will not be available for donation if you end up brain-dead on life support or die. And even *if* you are signed up to a registry, distraught and ill-informed family members often overrule those wishes anyway. *Presumed consent* simply reverses this, putting the onus on citizens to "opt out."

Presumed consent could raise the participation rate from the current 45 percent to as much as 97 percent.

Renowned bioethicist Arthur Caplan of the Hastings Center states,

> Spain, Italy, Austria, Belgium, and some other European countries have enacted laws that create presumed consent,

or what I prefer to call "default to donation." In such a system, the presumption is that you want to be an organ donor upon your death—the default to donation. People who don't want to be organ donors have to say so by registering this wish on a computer, carrying a card, or telling their loved ones. With default to donation, no one's rights are taken away—voluntary altruism remains the moral foundation for making organs available, and, therefore, procuring organs is consistent with medical ethics.

Anyone with a religious, ethical, philosophical—or even a random and unexplained—objection to being a donor need do nothing more than fill out a brief form in order to opt out. "Based on the European experience," Caplan explains, "there is a good chance America could get a significant jump in the supply of organs by shifting to a default-to-donation policy. Donation rates in European countries with presumed consent are about 25% higher than in other European nations."

Presumed consent could raise the participation rate from the current 45 percent to as much as 97 percent—almost exactly equivalent to the 95 percent of respondents in a 2005 Gallup poll who said they approved of organ donation. The policy would drastically reduce the complexity and expense of ongoing efforts for registration, creating awareness, and operational support of current registries.

An opt-out system would also improve the rate of family consent—discussed earlier—which is a critical factor in addressing the organ shortage. According to a 2005 study from scientists at Harvard and the University of Chicago, "Countries with an environment of presumed consent foster greater participation, and less objections, from the family members of potential donors."

"Awareness" campaigns are simply not enough, and signing up more donors to state registries, or to a national registry, will have only modest and incremental effects. Most states now have driver's license registries, and about 45 percent of adult Americans have signed up—yet the waiting lists grow daily. Andrew Cameron, MD, PhD, of the Johns Hopkins University School of Medicine in Baltimore, recently inspired Facebook to launch a new feature that "let users change their profile status to indicate 'organ donor.'" (Cameron had been roommates with Sheryl Sandberg, COO of Facebook, at Harvard.) The program led to a huge short-term spike in online registrations, but the results did not last, and it did not put a dent in the waiting lists. Cameron and Sandberg are to be applauded, but they need help from Congress.

In 1983, Cyclosporine (the first immunosuppressant anti-rejection drug) hit the market and organ transplantation quickly moved from the realm of science fiction to that of everyday medicine.

As Cameron told *Slate* last year, "The shortage of donated organs . . . is not a medical problem but a social problem." However, for new government initiatives or programs like Facebook's to be successful and drive the overall participation rate in organ donation registries significantly higher would require massive and sustained educational and logistical operations. Ongoing effectiveness would require long-term commitments, resources and a great deal of money—and it would still make little difference. Even a 25 percent or 50 percent improvement in participation would still pale compared to what we'd get with presumed consent. In countries where the onus is on citizens to opt out, only about 3 percent ever bother to do so—meaning 97 percent are donors.

Step 3: Get rid of the "God Committees"!

In 1983, Cyclosporine (the first immunosuppressant anti-rejection drug) hit the market and organ transplantation quickly moved from the realm of science fiction to that of everyday medicine. The number of successful transplants grew exponentially, but the number of eligible recipients started to grow even faster. So our government took action: In 1984, Congress passed the National Organ Transplant Act (NOTA), which created the Organ Procurement and Transplantation Network (OPTN) and called for it to be run by a private, nonprofit organization under federal contract. The federal "Final Rule" provides a regulatory framework for the structure and operation of the OPTN and mandates that it should:

- Increase and ensure the effectiveness, efficiency and equity of organ sharing in the national system of organ allocation,

- Increase the supply of donated organs available for transplantation

The United Network for Organ Sharing (UNOS) was first awarded the national OPTN contract by the U.S. Department of Health and Human Services in 1986. A quasi-governmental agency, UNOS continues today as the only organization ever to operate the OPTN. How is UNOS doing in their efforts to achieve those two primary goals? Well, the aggregated waiting list has skyrocketed from a few thousand names in the eighties to over a hundred and twenty thousand, and the average wait has grown from around one year to seven. Throughout the entire existence of UNOS, the desperate shortage of organs for American patients who need them has only worsened. There has been little in the way of an effective national awareness campaign and little has ever been done to substantially improve access to life-saving organs.

Furthermore, waiting lists at transplant centers around the country are not subjected to proper oversight to ensure more fair and less arbitrary distribution of precious life-saving organs. The committees that maintain the waiting lists at transplant centers around the country are known, colloquially, to some in the illegal organ trade as "God Committees." They have significant leeway in deciding who to move up or down their list, and their existence contributes to the fact that white people statistically get more organs per capita than black people, and rich people get more than the poor. Rich, white people also get more of the "better" organs (those sourced from living donors as opposed to those harvested from cadavers).

National standards need to be created for who gets placed on waiting lists, who gets moved up or down, and why, and they need to be enforced with active oversight.

According to a 2013 article in Nashville's *Tennessean*, "Although the number of blacks and whites waiting for a kidney in 2011 was about the same, whites received just over half of kidney transplants that year, while blacks received less than a third." A study in the *Clinical Journal of the American Society of Nephrology*, first published online in September of 2010, stated: "Living donor kidney transplant (LDKT) is usually the best treatment option for kidney failure but occurs less frequently among persons who are black or older. In 2007, blacks comprised only 13.8% of LDKT recipients in the United States—a percentage that has remained unchanged for 10 years. In contrast, blacks make up 30 percent to 40 percent of the dialysis population." The researchers go on to say that, "We were struck by the disparities by race and insurance type: African-Americans were much less likely to receive kidney transplantation prior to requiring dialytic support, as were those with public or no insurance."

The distribution of life-saving kidneys and other organs should not be left up to the individual "God committees" at the many transplant centers scattered around the country, each with its own set of rules and ability to deviate from those guidelines, arbitrarily, as its members see fit at any given moment. Whether the decision of who to move up, or down, on a waiting list is ever motivated by ill intent, somehow rooted in subconscious preferences or prejudices, or whether it is something else entirely, remains unknown.

There is, however, an ongoing inequity based on race and economic status. It needs to be investigated and addressed by the Department of Health and Human Services or a congressional committee. National standards need to be created for who gets placed on waiting lists, who gets moved up or down, and why, and they need to be enforced with active oversight.

The Need to Do Something

The ethical and philosophical questions that come up in any evaluation of organ transplantation and organ donations are a minefield of religious and ethical confusion and contradictions. Most major religions are strongly in favor of organ donations, and Pope John Paul II stated, "The Catholic Church would promote the fact that there is a need for organ donors and that Christians should accept this as a 'challenge to their generosity and fraternal love' so long as ethical principles are followed."

Under a system of presumed consent, those who object could simply opt out and would be unaffected by it. The people on those waiting lists need life-saving organs and right now there are rational, ethical, cost-saving and proven methods available to us of getting those needed organs to them. Even if presumed consent legislation doesn't wipe out a major portion of the organ shortage in America overnight—though it might—and it only saves a handful of lives, don't those lives matter enough to warrant some attention from one Republican and one Democratic member of Congress? For the 18 families who will lose a loved one today, it is worth a conversation.

In the coming years and decades most members of our current Congress will know at least one person who will suffer renal failure and will need a kidney to stay alive. Some of them will die waiting. And our leaders in government can—must—do something to prevent that from happening.

Cash for Kidneys: The Case for a Market for Organs

Gary S. Becker and Julio J. Elías

Gary S. Becker taught economics and sociology at the University of Chicago and at the Booth School of Business, and was a senior fellow at the Hoover Institution. Julio J. Elías is a professor of economics at the Universidad del CEMA in Argentina.

In 2012, 95,000 American men, women and children were on the waiting list for new kidneys, the most commonly transplanted organ. Yet only about 16,500 kidney transplant operations were performed that year. Taking into account the number of people who die while waiting for a transplant, this implies an average wait of 4.5 years for a kidney transplant in the U.S.

The situation is far worse than it was just a decade ago, when nearly 54,000 people were on the waiting list, with an average wait of 2.9 years. For all the recent attention devoted to the health-care overhaul, the long and growing waiting times for tens of thousands of individuals who badly need organ transplants hasn't been addressed.

Finding a way to increase the supply of organs would reduce wait times and deaths, and it would greatly ease the suffering that many sick individuals now endure while they hope for a transplant. The most effective change, we believe, would be to provide compensation to people who give their organs—that is, we recommend establishing a market for organs.

Organ transplants are one of the extraordinary developments of modern science. They began in 1954 with a kidney transplant performed at Brigham & Women's hospital in Boston. But the practice only took off in the 1970s with the development of immunosuppressive drugs that could prevent the rejection of transplanted organs. Since then, the number of kidney and other organ transplants has grown rapidly, but not nearly as rapidly as the growth in the number of people with defective organs who need transplants. The result has been longer and longer delays to receive organs.

Many of those waiting for kidneys are on dialysis, and life expectancy while on dialysis isn't long. For example, people age 45 to 49 live, on average, eight additional years if they remain on dialysis, but they live an additional 23 years if they get a kidney transplant. That is why in 2012, almost 4,500 persons died while waiting for kidney transplants. Although some of those waiting would have died anyway, the great majority died because they were unable to replace their defective kidneys quickly enough.

Exhortations and other efforts to encourage more organ donations have failed to significantly close the large gap between supply and demand.

The toll on those waiting for kidneys and on their families is enormous, from both greatly reduced life expectancy and the many hardships of being on dialysis. Most of those on dialysis cannot work, and the annual cost of dialysis averages about $80,000. The total cost over the average 4.5-year waiting period before receiving a kidney transplant is $350,000, which is much larger than the $150,000 cost of the transplant itself.

Individuals can live a normal life with only one kidney, so about 34% of all kidneys used in transplants come from live donors. The majority of transplant kidneys come from parents, children, siblings and other relatives of those who need transplants. The rest come from individuals who want to help those in need of transplants.

In recent years, kidney exchanges—in which pairs of living would-be donors and recipients who prove incompatible look for another pair or pairs of donors and recipients who would be compatible for transplants, cutting their wait time—have become more widespread. Although these exchanges have grown rapidly in the U.S. since 2005, they still account for only 9% of live donations and just 3% of all kidney donations, including after-death donations. The relatively minor role of exchanges in total donations isn't an accident, because exchanges are really a form of barter, and barter is always an inefficient way to arrange transactions.

Exhortations and other efforts to encourage more organ donations have failed to significantly close the large gap between supply and demand. For example, some countries use an implied consent approach, in which organs from cadavers are assumed to be available for transplant unless, before death, individuals indicate that they don't want their organs to be used. (The U.S. continues to use informed consent, requiring people to make an active declaration of their wish to donate.) In our own highly preliminary study of a few countries—Argentina, Austria, Brazil, Chile and Denmark—that have made the shift to implied consent from informed consent or vice versa, we found that the switch didn't lead to consistent changes in the number of transplant surgeries.

Other studies have found more positive effects from switching to implied consent, but none of the effects would be large enough to eliminate the sizable shortfall in the supply of organs in the U.S. That shortfall isn't just an American problem. It exists in most other countries as well, even when they use different methods to procure organs and have different cultures and traditions.

Paying donors for their organs would finally eliminate the supply-demand gap. In particular, sufficient payment to kidney donors would increase the supply of kidneys by a large percentage, without greatly increasing the total cost of a kidney transplant.

We have estimated how much individuals would need to be paid for kidneys to be willing to sell them for transplants. These estimates take account of the slight risk to donors from transplant surgery, the number of weeks of work lost during the surgery and recovery periods, and the small risk of reduction in the quality of life.

Since the number of kidneys available at a reasonable price would be far more than needed to close the gap between the demand and supply of kidneys, there would no longer be any significant waiting time to get a kidney transplant.

Our conclusion is that a very large number of both live and cadaveric kidney donations would be available by paying about $15,000 for each kidney. That estimate isn't exact, and the true cost could be as high as $25,000 or as low as $5,000— but even the high estimate wouldn't increase the total cost of kidney transplants by a large percentage.

Few countries have ever allowed the open purchase and sale of organs, but Iran permits the sale of kidneys by living donors. Scattered and incomplete evidence from Iran indicates that the price of kidneys there is about $4,000 and that waiting times to get kidneys have been largely eliminated. Since Iran's per capita income is one-quarter of that of the U.S., this evidence supports our $15,000 estimate. Other countries are also starting to think along these lines: Singapore and Australia have recently introduced limited payments to live donors that compensate mainly for time lost from work.

Since the number of kidneys available at a reasonable price would be far more than needed to close the gap between the demand and supply of kidneys, there would no longer be any significant waiting time to get a kidney transplant. The number of people on dialysis would decline dramatically, and deaths due to long waits for a transplant would essentially disappear.

Today, finding a compatible kidney isn't easy. There are four basic blood types, and tissue matching is complex and involves the combination of six proteins. Blood and tissue type determine the chance that a kidney will help a recipient in the long run. But the sale of organs would result in a large supply of most kidney types, and with large numbers of kidneys available, transplant surgeries could be arranged to suit the health of recipients (and donors) because surgeons would be confident that compatible kidneys would be available.

The system that we're proposing would include payment to individuals who agree that their organs can be used after they die. This is important because transplants for heart and lungs and most liver transplants only use organs from the deceased. Under a new system, individuals would sell their organs "forward" (that is, for future use), with payment going to their heirs after their organs are harvested. Relatives sometimes refuse to have organs used even when a deceased family member has explicitly requested it, and they would be more inclined to honor such wishes if they received substantial compensation for their assent.

Any claim about the supposed immorality of organ sales should be weighed against the morality of preventing thousands of deaths each year and improving the quality of life of those waiting for organs.

The idea of paying organ donors has met with strong opposition from some (but not all) transplant surgeons and other doctors, as well as various academics, political leaders and others. Critics have claimed that paying for organs would be ineffective, that payment would be immoral because it involves the sale of body parts and that the main donors would be the desperate poor, who could come to regret their decision. In short, critics believe that monetary payments for organs would be repugnant.

But the claim that payments would be ineffective in eliminating the shortage of organs isn't consistent with what we know about the supply of other parts of the body for medical use. For example, the U.S. allows market-determined payments to surrogate mothers—and surrogacy takes time, involves great discomfort and is somewhat risky. Yet in the U.S., the average payment to a surrogate mother is only about $20,000.

Another illuminating example is the all-volunteer U.S. military. Critics once asserted that it wouldn't be possible to get enough capable volunteers by offering them only reasonable pay, especially in wartime. But the all-volunteer force has worked well in the U.S., even during wars, and the cost of these recruits hasn't been excessive.

Whether paying donors is immoral because it involves the sale of organs is a much more subjective matter, but we question this assertion, given the very serious problems with the present system. Any claim about the supposed immorality of organ sales should be weighed against the morality of preventing thousands of deaths each year and improving the quality of life of those waiting for organs. How can paying for organs to increase their supply be more immoral than the injustice of the present system?

Under the type of system we propose, safeguards could be created against impulsive behavior or exploitation. For example, to reduce the likelihood of rash donations, a period of three months or longer could be required before someone would be allowed to donate their kidneys or other organs. This would give donors a chance to re-evaluate their decisions, and they could change their minds at any time before the surgery. They could also receive guidance from counselors on the wisdom of these decisions.

Though the poor would be more likely to sell their kidneys and other organs, they also suffer more than others from the current scarcity. Today, the rich often don't wait as long as others for organs since some of them go to countries such as India, where they can arrange for transplants in the underground medical sector, and others (such as the late Steve Jobs) manage to jump the queue by having residence in several states or other means. The sale of organs would make them more available to the poor, and Medicaid could help pay for the added cost of transplant surgery.

Over time . . . the sale of organs would grow to be accepted, just as the voluntary military now has widespread support.

The altruistic giving of organs might decline with an open market, since the incentive to give organs to a relative, friend or anyone else would be weaker when organs are readily available to buy. On the other hand, the altruistic giving of money to those in need of organs could increase to help them pay for the cost of organ transplants.

Paying for organs would lead to more transplants—and thereby, perhaps, to a large increase in the overall medical costs of transplantation. But it would save the cost of dialysis for people waiting for kidney transplants and other costs to individuals waiting for other organs. More important, it would prevent thousands of deaths and improve the quality of life among those who now must wait years before getting the organs they need.

Initially, a market in the purchase and sale of organs would seem strange, and many might continue to consider that market "repugnant." Over time, however, the sale of organs would grow to be accepted, just as the voluntary military now has widespread support.

Eventually, the advantages of allowing payment for organs would become obvious. At that point, people will wonder why it took so long to adopt such an obvious and sensible solution to the shortage of organs for transplant.

Organ Transplants Should Be Rare and Not for Gain

Miran Epstein

Miran Epstein is senior lecturer in medical ethics and law at Barts and The London School of Medicine and Dentistry, Queen Mary College, University of London.

Organ transplantation is one of the most impressive achievements of modern medicine. It has brought hope to millions of patients suffering from previously fatal organ failure. For many, it has made life longer and better.

It has benefited many professionals and industries, too, by becoming a new source of pride, funding, and profit. Struggling to contain costs, health-care payers are also among its beneficiaries. Kidney transplantation, for example, has proved to be less costly than dialysis.

Yet, since its inception, transplant medicine has been grappling with a rapidly increasing gap between the supply of organs and demand for them. For most stakeholders, the often dire consequences gave rise to a whole set of solutions, all based on one general strategy: if we are short of organs, then let us get more of them.

The Slippery Slope of Transplant Ethics

This strategy has come with a high price tag, however. On the one hand, it has given rise to some exceptionally corrupt practices, such as organ trafficking, transplant tourism, and many other ugly phenomena associated with a black market in organs. On the other hand, it has put transplant ethics under severe strain.

Indeed, transplant ethics has been on a slippery slope almost since transplants began. The strategy of getting more organs has pushed, and continues to push, the ethical line to places that had previously been deemed immoral.

To tackle insufficient supply from the dead, we first embraced an increasingly inclusive, and at any rate flexible, definition of death. This has often raised suspicions about the motivations of doctors in pronouncing a candidate donor's death.

We then came up with the idea of opt-out consent for deceased organ donation. This system, which allows organs to be harvested also from refusers who have failed to express their refusal, has not increased trust in medicine, either.

Those in need of organs or money [would] likely . . . turn to the black market or seek a legal loophole that would allow them to conceal the commercial transaction behind some legitimate gesture.

As the organ crisis continued to deepen, we allowed donations from the living. This was particularly audacious, for it required us to abandon the supreme Hippocratic principle according to which it is unprofessional to injure a healthy person.

The Expansion of Living Donations

In the category of living donations, we first permitted only directed donations by relatives and non-directed donations by non-relatives. We assumed that family ties and non-directedness would preclude coercion and commerce. However, the mechanisms we used to confirm that assumption were conveniently lax. They did not allow certain forms of coercion to interfere with the donor's consent. Nor were they overly fastidious about clandestine commercial ties.

By that time, we had already become aware that interests in organ commerce were constantly intensifying, and that those in need of organs or money were increasingly likely to turn to the black market or seek a legal loophole that would allow them to conceal the commercial transaction behind some legitimate gesture. Until recently, we have not done much about the black market (the 2008 Declaration of Istanbul marks the beginning of a determined struggle against this market), but we banned altruistic directed donations by living non-relatives out of fear that they would become that legal loophole.

This fear did not last long, though. The increasing demand for more organs has driven us to legitimize this category as well. Indeed, it has helped a lot, but it has not sufficed, either.

Currently, we peddle the idea of quasi-non-commercial incentives for organ donations from both the deceased and the living. For example, the new Israeli transplant law provides incentives for people to sign a donor card by giving them and their relatives priority on transplant waiting lists. This material incentive is in clear breach of the principle that organs should be distributed according to need only. Moreover, it is likely to discriminate against people who are either unaware of the donor-card system or tend to refuse to sign the card for reasons associated with religious beliefs or low trust in the medical authorities.

The same law indeed forbids commerce in organs, but offers living donors reimbursement of expenses that contains fixed-sum elements. Moreover, the Israeli National Transplant and Organ Donation Center now openly encourages providers, insurance companies, and the Donor Card Institution, to pay families who consent to donate the organs of their deceased relative. Such arrangements, which should be described as government-sponsored commercialism, are considered unacceptable by all relevant international declarations.

The Sale of Organs

If things continue as they have, we will soon become tired of quick-fix remedies. Indeed, advocates of the increasingly popular idea of a regulated market in organs claim that it is the ultimate treatment. Perhaps it is. But let us not even go there! For even if we believe that buyers and sellers of organs can in principle enter the transaction on the basis of free choice, none of them has chosen to face the underlying dilemma in the first place.

Both are victims: the buyer is a victim of morbidity and declining social solidarity, while the seller is a victim of poverty and other forms of financial distress. A regulated market would not challenge these man-made facts. Instead, it would reaffirm them more than any previous ethical solution has ever done.

Many of the social crises that we currently face are just symptoms. Yet the underlying problems must be addressed as well if we are to lead the kind of life that human beings can and deserve to have. The organ crisis is no different. Instead of medicalizing and ethicalizing it, let us direct our main efforts at draining the swamp. Organ transplantation, like mosquito repellent, should be used sparingly, and only when there is no other choice.

The Dead-Donor Rule Is Ethically Central to Organ Donation

L. Syd M. Johnson

L. Syd M. Johnson is an assistant professor of philosophy and bioethics at Michigan Technological University.

The success of organ transplantation has given rise to a perpetual shortage of lifesaving organs. In the US and Canada, thousands of people die on waiting lists each year because there are never enough organ donors for all the potential recipients. Despite overwhelming public support for organ donation, not everyone opts to be a donor, and not every family consents to posthumous donation. Misconceptions and a lack of accurate information about organ donation account in part for the disparity between support for donation and actual willingness to donate. Current organ procurement practices may foster some of those misconceptions and discourage organ donation.

The Dead Donor Rule

A central ethical precept for organ donation is the Dead Donor Rule, which requires that persons must be dead before organs and tissues are removed from their bodies. This ensures that living but incapacitated persons are not killed by the removal of their vital organs. In Canada and the United States, there are two possible ways to legally determine death in organ donors: brain death and cardiac death.

Brain dead patients are the source of most cadaver organs because for organs to remain healthy and suitable for transplantation, they must be perfused with blood and oxygen. The hearts of brain dead patients beat spontaneously, even during the removal of organs, so maintaining healthy organs requires only that oxygen and fluids be provided until the organs are procured. Organs become damaged and nonviable soon after circulation stops, so the organs of persons who die of cardiac arrest are usually not suitable for transplantation. There is persistent confusion and misunderstanding amongst the public about brain death, pointing to a need not only for better education, but also more clarity and honesty from the medical community about the difference between brain death and death as it is traditionally understood.

Across cultures and religious traditions, there is wide agreement and acceptance that death occurs when the heart stops. According to most legal criteria for cardiac death, it is the *irreversible* cessation of cardiac function that defines death. The interval needed to determine when cardiac function has irreversibly stopped is lengthy because some patients can be successfully resuscitated several minutes—even half an hour—after the heart stops.

Donation After Cardiac Death

In a practice known as Donation After Cardiac Death, life support is withdrawn from an organ donor, death is declared soon after the heart stops, and the organs are quickly harvested.

The important goal of increasing organ donation cannot be achieved without addressing the problem of donation resistance caused by a lack of trust.

Like all organ donations, Donation After Cardiac Death is done *only* with the consent of the patient's family. The practice is controversial because the length of time before death is declared is determined not by the impossibility of resuscitating the patient, but by the desire to preserve the organs for donation. The length of that interval varies greatly from country to country, province to province, and even between hospitals, resulting in a lack of standardization and uniformity. Moreover, death is declared without a determination that cardiac function has ceased *irreversibly*, so Donation After Cardiac Death may violate the Dead Donor Rule, because the donor is not dead according to legally accepted standards. While Donation After Cardiac Death increases the number of lifesaving organs available for transplant, it does so by fudging the determination of death. It may not necessarily be ethically wrong to withdraw life support and harvest organs when there is informed family consent; however, the lack of uniform and transparent standards for declaring death before donation creates the perception of medical deception.

The lack of transparency about death before donation erodes public trust in the activities of the medical profession when it comes to organ donation. In surveys, potential donors express the concern that organs could be unethically or prematurely procured, whether intentionally or as a result of mistakes. Others identify doubts about the concept of brain death as a barrier to becoming a willing donor. Non-donors also consistently express the fear that they'll receive substandard or less aggressive medical treatment, or that their willingness to be an organ donor might result in their premature, preventable death.

These worries are not allayed by organ procurement practices that appear to push ethical boundaries, or rest on definitions of death that are gerrymandered to serve the needs of transplantation. The important goal of increasing organ donation cannot be achieved without addressing the problem of donation resistance caused by a lack of trust. Greater honesty and transparency on the part of the medical community about death before donation would benefit the public—including those waiting for transplants—by instilling confidence in a system that serves the needs of both the living and the dying.

The Dead-Donor Rule and the Future of Organ Donation

Robert D. Truog, Franklin G. Miller, and Scott D. Halpern

Robert D. Truog is professor of medical ethics, anesthesiology, and pediatrics at Harvard Medical School; Franklin G. Miller is a member of the senior faculty in the department of bioethics at the National Institutes of Health; and Scott D. Halpern is assistant professor of medicine, epidemiology, and medical ethics and health policy at the Perelman School of Medicine, University of Pennsylvania.

The ethics of organ transplantation have been premised on "the dead-donor rule" (DDR), which states that vital organs should be taken only from persons who are dead. Yet it is not obvious why certain living patients, such as those who are near death but on life support, should not be allowed to donate their organs, if doing so would benefit others and be consistent with their own interests.

This issue is not merely theoretical. In one recent case, the parents of a young girl wanted to donate her organs after an accident had left her with devastating brain damage. Plans were made to withdraw life support and to procure her organs shortly after death. But the attempt to donate was aborted because the girl did not die quickly enough to allow procurement of viable organs. Her parents experienced this failure to donate as a second loss; they questioned why their daughter could not have been given an anesthetic and had the organs removed before life support was stopped. As another parent of a donor child observed when confronted by the limitations of the DDR, "There was no chance at all that our daughter was going to survive. . . . I can follow the ethicist's argument, but it seems totally ludicrous."

In another recent case described by Dr. Joseph Darby at the University of Pittsburgh Medical Center, the family of a man with devastating brain injury requested withdrawal of life support. The man had been a strong advocate of organ donation, but he was not a candidate for any of the traditional approaches. His family therefore sought permission for him to donate organs before death. To comply with the DDR, plans were made to remove only nonvital organs (a kidney and a lobe of the liver) while he was under anesthesia and then take him back to the intensive care unit, where life support would be withdrawn. Although the plan was endorsed by the clinical team, the ethics committee, and the hospital administration, it was not honored because multiple surgeons who were contacted refused to recover the organs: the rules of the United Network for Organ Sharing (UNOS) state that the patient must give direct consent for living donation, which this patient's neurologic injury rendered impossible. Consequently, he died without the opportunity to donate. If there were no requirement to comply with the DDR, the family would have been permitted to donate all the patient's vital organs.

By blocking reasonable requests from patients and families to donate, the [Dead-Donor Rule] both infringes donor autonomy and unnecessarily limits the number and quality of transplantable organs.

Allegiance to the DDR thus limits the procurement of transplantable organs by denying some patients the option to donate in situations in which death is imminent and donation is desired. But the problems with the DDR go deeper than that. The DDR has required physicians and society to develop criteria for declaring patients dead while their organs are still alive. The first response to this challenge was development of the concept of brain death. Patients meeting criteria for brain death were originally considered to be dead because they had lost "the integrated functioning of the organism as a whole," a scientific definition of life reflecting the basic biologic concept of homeostasis. Over the past several decades, however, it has become clear that patients diagnosed as brain dead have not lost this homeostatic balance but can maintain extensive integrated functioning for years. Even though brain death is not compatible with a scientific understanding of death, its wide acceptance suggests that other factors help to justify recovery of organs. For example, brain-dead patients are permanently unconscious and cannot live without a ventilator. Recovery of their organs is therefore considered acceptable if organ donation is desired by the patient or by the surrogate on the patient's behalf.

More recently, to meet the ever-growing need for transplantable organs, attention has turned to donors who are declared dead on the basis of the irreversible loss of circulatory function. Here again, we struggle with the need to declare death when organs are still viable for transplantation. This requirement has led to rules permitting organ procurement after the patient has been pulseless for at least 2 minutes. Yet for many such patients, circulatory function is not yet irreversibly lost within this timeframe—cardiopulmonary resuscitation could restore it. So a compromise has been reached whereby organ procurement may begin before the loss of circulation is known to be irreversible, provided that clinicians wait long enough to have confidence that the heart will not restart on its own, and the patient or surrogate agrees that resuscitation will not be attempted (since such an attempt could result in a patient's being "brought back to life" after having been declared dead).

Reasonable people could hardly be faulted for viewing these compromises as little more than medical charades. We therefore suggest that a sturdier foundation for the ethics of organ transplantation can be found in two fundamental ethical principles: autonomy and nonmaleficence. Respect for a utonomy requires that people be given choices in the circumstances of their dying, including donating organs. Nonmaleficence requires protecting patients from harm. Accordingly, patients should be permitted to donate vital organs except in circumstances in which doing so would harm them; and they would not be harmed when their death was imminent owing to a decision to stop life support. That patients be dead before their organs are recovered is not a foundational ethical requirement. Rather, by blocking reasonable requests from patients and families to donate, the DDR both infringes donor autonomy and unnecessarily limits the number and quality of transplantable organs.

When death is very near, some patients may want to die in the process of helping others to live, even if that means altering the timing or manner of their death.

Many observers nevertheless insist that the DDR must be upheld to maintain public trust in the organ-transplantation enterprise. However, the limited available evidence suggests that a sizeable proportion of the public is less concerned about the timing of death in organ donation than about the process of decision making and assurances that the patient will not recover—concerns that are compatible with an ethical focus on autonomy and nonmaleficence.

Although shifting the ethical foundation of organ donation from the DDR to the principles of autonomy and nonmaleficence would require creation of legal exceptions to our homicide laws, this would not be the first time we have struggled to reconcile laws with the desire of individual patients to die in the manner of their own choosing. In the 1970s, patients won the right to have ventilator use and other forms of life support discontinued, despite physicians' arguments that doing so would constitute unlawful killing. Since that time, physicians have played an active role in decisions about whether and when life support should be withdrawn, and the willingness of physicians to accept this active role in the dying process has probably enhanced, rather than eroded, the public trust in the profession.

Our society generally supports the view that people should be granted the broadest range of freedoms compatible with assurance of the same for others. Some people may have personal moral views that preclude the approach we describe here, and these views should be respected. Nevertheless, the views of people who may freely avoid these options provide no basis for denying such liberties to those who wish to pursue them. When death is very near, some patients may want to die in the process of helping others to live, even if that means altering the timing or manner of their death. We believe that policymakers should take these citizens' requests seriously and begin to engage in a discussion about abandoning the DDR.

A Kidney for a Kidney

Sally Satel

Sally Satel is a psychiatrist and resident scholar at the American Enterprise Institute.

Last month [March 2013], the Senate Health, Education, Labor and Pensions Committee made life a little better for people awaiting an organ transplant. It passed the HIV Organ Policy Equity (HOPE) Act, legislation designed to end the federal ban on research into organ donations from deceased HIV-positive donors to HIV-positive recipients. It would permit the Secretary of Health and Human Services to sanction such transplant operations if the research establishes their safety.

"Those infected with HIV are now living much longer and, as a consequence, are suffering more kidney and liver failure," said Sen. Tom Coburn, a physician and one of the bill's co-sponsors. Advocates of the legislation, which has bipartisan support in the House, estimate that organs from deceased HIV-positive donors could each year save about 1,000 HIV-infected patients who suffer from liver and kidney failure.

The future beneficiaries of HOPE aren't just the patients desperate for a new kidney, liver, or heart. The donors also benefit; they see value in leaving their organs to medicine. Giving the "gift of life," the narrative long championed by the transplant community to encourage people to become donors, is an opportunity to perform the ultimate charitable act— saving the life of another. Through posthumous donation, some people see the chance to fulfill a moral obligation to help others or to make something life-affirming come from their death.

Organ Donation by Prison Inmates

Another marked population—prison inmates—is also pushing to expand its opportunity to save lives. Last month, Utah state legislator Steve Eliason proposed a bill allowing prisoners to sign up to become donors if their death occurs while incarcerated.

Although there is currently no nationwide legal proscription against prisoners signing up to become posthumous donors, Eliason wanted the allowance enshrined in statute. "There are many inmates who are constantly looking to give back to society in any way they can," said Steven Gehrke of the Utah Department of Corrections, which supports Eliason's effort. "They feel like sitting in prison doesn't really repay their debts." At least three other states—Arizona, Texas, and California—promote deceased donation among inmates.

But what about inmates who want to donate while they are still alive?

I have not been able to find any states that permit inmates to give a kidney to a stranger.

In December 2011, I received a letter from Shannon Ross, 29, at the Stanley Correctional Institution in Wisconsin. He is eight years into a 17-year sentence for reckless homicide. Ross, who had read an article I wrote about the country's organ shortage, had a simple request:

"I am hoping you can give me some advice about my desire to get the state [of Wisconsin] to allow inmates to donate their organs—without compensation. . . . I am not simply looking to be humored as I try to make my time pass faster. I have been pursuing this objective for five years now."

Ross wanted to donate one of his kidneys to a stranger. And he wanted to do it now, given the odds that his organs would no longer be usable after he died.

Ross had done his homework. He pointed out that a patient who receives a kidney from a live donor instead of a cadaver can expect the organ to last several years longer. He knew that the operation he would undergo involved the surgeon making a few keyhole-size incisions in the abdomen and that the hospital stay is usually two days. Ross said this was not a decision he made lightly—surgery is not a trivial event—but stressed that he would want to donate even if the recovery period were more prolonged.

The barrier was the penal system. "As a rule, we are banned from live organ donation (even though an inmate in need of an organ is given equal priority on the waiting list as everyone else)," Ross wrote me some months later. Wisconsin's department of corrections is not alone in imposing such a ban on prisoners; I have not been able to find any states that permit inmates to give a kidney to a stranger. This stance mirrors the policy of the Federal Bureau of Prisons, which forbids federal inmates to donate to a stranger. The Bureau does, however, allow live organ and bone marrow donation by federal inmates when the recipient is a parent, sibling, or biological child.

Safe and Fair Inmate Donation

In my view, there is no compelling reason to bar all inmates, as a matter of policy, from making live donations to strangers. Bioethicists may contend that it is not ethical to allow prisoners to donate because incarceration is a coercive process that limits one's freedom to make a choice, but there are ways to make inmate donation safe and fair. For example, authorities would stipulate that the donation could not have bearing on parole, and the donor would be made fully aware that relinquishing an organ would do nothing to secure early release.

What's more, a prospective donor would undergo rigorous informed consent regarding surgery and the risks of living with one kidney, as is required for any kidney donor. Medical and psychological testing would be performed, which is also standard. A several-month "cooling off" period before surgery should be a good gauge of an inmate's commitment to donate. Likewise, review by a prison-appointed panel could determine the authenticity of his request as well as a test of whether his expectations are realistic. Annual medical checkups following transplant could be paid through a Medicaid voucher (which is not even a regular feature of standard donation on "the outside").

With roughly 117,000 people waiting for an organ, inmate donation would still be a most welcome contribution to public health.

Hepatitis and HIV occur at relatively high rates in the prison population, posing a risk of transmitting the diseases to non-infected recipients. But the solution is to test the inmate at initial screening—the standard procedure for any living donor—and then again at three weeks prior to surgery. He should be kept in medical isolation between the final test and the transplant date so he can't become infected and pass on a newly acquired virus before it can be detected.

This strategy would provide as much, if not more, confidence in the safety of the transplant as is the case for standard transplants. Compare this to the procedure surrounding unplanned, deceased donors—often victims of gunshot wounds or car accidents—where there is pressure to obtain test results quickly, to rely on family members for donors' health information, and to perform the transplant before the removed cadaver organ becomes damaged from sitting "on ice" too long.

The impact of donation, both living and deceased, by inmates would probably be modest—perhaps a few hundred organs per year at most. Realistically, many organs from inmates would not be acceptable due to infectious disease. (Though if HOPE passes, more HIV-positive organs will be eligible for transplantation to people who are already infected.)

But with roughly 117,000 people waiting for an organ, inmate donation would still be a most welcome contribution to public health. Besides saving lives—virtue enough—it could also help the cause of justice. "After how much we have taken from society," Ross told me, "it's unacceptable that society is denied the opportunity to receive something so valuable from us in return."

Condemned Prisoners Should Not Be Able to Donate Organs After Execution

Wesley J. Smith

Wesley J. Smith is a senior fellow at the Discovery Institute's Center on Human Exceptionalism and consults for the Patients Rights Council and the Center for Bioethics and Culture.

We have discussed here the drive with bioethics and transplant medicine to kill and harvest organs from people in a persistently unconscious condition. We have discussed how euthanasia and organ donation are now coupled in Belgium. And we have discussed how Jack Kevorkian, before turning to the sick and disabled, went from prison to prison asking to use condemned prisoners in medical experiments during executions, in which the killing process would be slowed so he could dig around in their bodies before they died.

Now, the *New York Times* has an opinion piece by a condemned prisoner promoting organ donation from people on death row. From "Giving Life After Death Row," by Christian Longo;

> EIGHT years ago I was sentenced to death for the murders of my wife and three children. I am guilty. I once thought that I could fool others into believing this was not true. Failing that, I tried to convince myself that it didn't matter. But gradually, the enormity of what I did seeped in; that was followed by remorse and then a wish to make amends. I spend 22 hours a day locked in a 6 foot by 8 foot box on Oregon's death row. There is no way to atone for my crimes,

but I believe that a profound benefit to society can come from my circumstances. I have asked to end my remaining appeals, and then donate my organs after my execution to those who need them. But my request has been rejected by the prison authorities.

Sorry, society should not be twisted in a utilitarian direction so Longo can assuage his guilt or give his life purpose.

If we ever start killing people for their organs, we will have opened a Pandora's box that will never close.

Think very carefully about this. Do we want the society *to have an increased stake in executing prisoners?* No. Even if one is for the death penalty, the issue should be strictly limited to crime and punishment. *Do we want prisoners deciding to give up appeals early*—as here—so their organs are more uselful, because even if they win, they face life in prison? No. Such a system could subtly skew the system against justice and toward the view that the organs of these murderers matter more than their lives. It could also impact other condemned prisoners depressed or bored on death row, who would be celebrated if they decided to allow themselves to be killed for their organs—as the adamantly anti-death penalty *Times* is facilitating by publishing this piece. Ah, the noble wife and family killer!

If I donated all of my organs today, I could clear nearly 1 percent of my state's organ waiting list. I am 37 years old and healthy; throwing my organs away after I am executed is nothing but a waste. And yet the prison authority's response to my latest appeal to donate was this: "The interests of the public and condemned inmates are best served by denying the petition."

The prison is right. This would be terrible for society. The utilitarian ethic that I think is slowly poisoning our culture would seep into other areas of criminal justice. What, for example, if a prisoner in for life without possibility of parole wanted to die to benefit society—with the added benefit of money saved! Moreover, once some of us were so treated, the logic of the thing would quickly leap to the fields of medicine and health care—adding impetus to viewing some people as so many organ systems particularly in the areas of assisted suicide/euthanasia and the food and fluids cases.

If we ever start killing people for their organs, we will have opened a Pandora's box that will never close. This is a Siren song.

Post Script: Secondhand Smokette [blog commenter] believes that anytime the fate of a convicted murderer is discussed, the victims should be named lest they become abstract and dehumanized. She is absolutely right and I was remiss in this post. Their names were wife, Mary Jane, 34, and their children Zachery, 4, Sadie, 3, and Madison, 2. He murdered them so he could lead a more lavish lifestyle.

CHAPTER 3

Are Reproductive Technologies Ethical?

Overview:
Reproductive Technologies
and Social Controversy

Anne Kingsley

Anne Kingsley is an English and literature instructor at Diablo Valley College in California.

In 1978 Louise Brown became the first "test tube" baby to be born using in vitro fertilization (IVF). Her birth marked the advent of a rapidly advancing reproductive science, and it also became a testament to a changing concept of creation. Her birth was not only a moment of celebration but also one of controversy. For some, IVF opposed traditional or religious beliefs about family and reproduction. Conception took place outside the body and outside the family and was altered through medical intervention. Many of the practices used in IVF and other assisted reproduction technologies (ART) challenged what was commonly thought of as the standard or normal family: one mother, one father, and children. A process such as egg or sperm donation, both of which take a third-party donor to create a fertilized embryo that will then be introduced into the female body using IVF, was therefore seen as counter to traditional family ideology and practice.

The success of IVF, however, opened new possibilities in the treatment of infertility. Proponents continued to see the practice as a means of conceiving a child where it otherwise may not have been possible. Many women who sought the treatment also supported this notion, considering the ability to conceive a child as their right. Today, the predominant public attitude toward assisted reproduction has shifted from wavering opposition to general acceptance. It is widely recognized and practiced as a standard treatment for infertility.

The increasing tendency to treat reproduction and conception as a medical issue has changed the traditional social narrative of the family.

The Controversies About Reproductive Technologies

The phenomenal increase in the number of babies born using alternative methods of fertilization over the past 20 years testifies to the changing outlook on once controversial medical procedures. Furthermore, the demand for reproductive options opens the door to more avenues of scientific exploration to both refine existing reproductive technologies and search for new methods. Accompanying the unprecedented rate of scientific growth, however, is a growing concern over the extent of new plateaus in reproductive technology and their costs. As a result, a new set of controversies and a new set of medical, ethical, and social questions have emerged to shape debate over assisted reproduction.

The new story of reproduction is located at the intersection of shifting social values and a rapidly advancing scientific understanding. New technologies afford women the decision to postpone reproduction. Hypothetically, a woman in her thirties, working toward a successful career or further education, is well aware that with each year the possibility of having a healthy child and an uncomplicated pregnancy diminishes. She is also aware that alternative procedures such as freezing one's eggs give her the tentative option of conceiving at a chosen future date. The process does not guarantee reproduction, but it does open new considerations in terms of family planning. In a society where fertility and pregnancy are at odds with "career ladders" for women, proponents of new advancements in reproductive technology see it as affording more lifestyle and body choices without sacrificing the desire to also have a family.

Yet skeptics argue that the original design of the fertility treatment was meant to offer infertility options, not lifestyle choices. A controversy over age limits emerges in this conversation because some critics worry how far medical practice will go to allow older women to conceive, even after menopause. Since ART is a relatively unregulated field of practice, no restrictions in age exist thus far. Many of these questions carry both scientific and social implications. On the one hand, reproductive technology has allowed women at many age levels to conceive and start a family. On the other hand, the increasing tendency to treat reproduction and conception as a medical issue has changed the traditional social narrative of the family. As prevalent as many of these controversies may be, their lack of resolution has not slowed the accelerating pace of further research and development.

New advancements and research in assisted reproductive technologies seek to make existing procedures more successful and more available to larger numbers of women. Newer processes mark not only how far we have come but also how far we may yet go. Advancements in reproductive technology create new controversies, many of which remain unaddressed.

The Risks and Benefits of Reproductive Technologies

One of the predominant issues with infertility treatments is the long-term effect on both the woman and the child. As standard as many of the procedures in ART are, long-term results are relatively unstudied. After all, Louise Brown, who turned 30 in 2008, is still relatively young. New measures are being taken to set up systems of surveillance that track and record the progress, the effects, and the health of the constituents involved. Some critics question how far we should advance medicine without knowing the full set of risks to mother and child. Proponents of the advancement in reproductive technologies see such suspicion of potential risks as a means of limiting female choice, undercutting the availability of IVF.

Scientific research and its applications must be carefully understood and monitored for its ethical and moral implications.

One of the known complications of ART is the predominance of multiple births. To ensure that pregnancy takes place, multiple embryos can be placed within the woman's uterus, potentially resulting in multiple births. Newer technologies can help predetermine healthy embryos, thus reducing the possibility of multiple births before implantation takes place. Yet the same technology used to prescreen the embryos can also be applied to screening for a predisposition to genetic diseases and for sex. The prescreening allows the parents to make decisions before fetal pregnancy occurs. The process of prescreening and selection of healthy embryos raises questions about the role of medical selection and the alteration of life outside the body. Some critics fear that the list of prescreening traits may grow longer, resulting in the institution of *Brave New World* tactics, where "designer babies" and "designer families" are the results of "quality control."

Interestingly, one of the more pressing quandaries generated by ART is its proximity to cloning. The laboratory techniques generated by ART are the same as those used in cloning. However, in a process such as IVF, the fertilized egg is the result of two biological parents, whereas with cloning, the cloned cell is the exact copy of one parent. Regulations controlling both cloning and stem cell research may also pose restrictions to ART, given that all are seen as working within the embryonic stages of life.

New advancements in reproductive technology carry risks along with the benefits. Although the technology is often heralded as necessary progress, critics point out that progress must be accompanied by bioethical responsibility. In other words, scientific research and its applications must be carefully understood and monitored for its ethical and moral implications.

The Issue of Bioethical Responsibility

Much of the current controversy in ART involves larger institutional practices rather than simply the medical procedures themselves. One such concern is the disposal of unused embryos. Here, the controversy intersects with the dialogue concerning post-coital contraceptive practices (such as the morning-after pill) and research practices in stem cell research—where does life begin? Proponents see the unused embryos, especially in stem cell research, as an opportunity for developing new treatments against disease. Opponents of using or destroying embryos, however, express concern over the increased power for science to manipulate fundamental definitions of life. Some critics even fear that the line between ethical and unethical practice gets ever more slippery as the limitations of embryonic research are further extended. Thus, ART again comes under scrutiny, requiring that more attention be given to regulations and limitations.

[Assisted reproduction technology] is a $3-billion-a-year industry at the intersection of medical practice and private business.

In order to address bioethical responsibility in assisted reproductive technology, some critics call for new measures in regulation. Those who call for regulation wish to monitor research practices more closely, including experimenting with new forms and methods of ART and medical practices actively applying existing methods of ART. Some women fear that "regulation" will equate to "restriction" of bodily rights, however, and certainly, determining bodily rights versus moral concerns is a difficult process.

An issue that may be overlooked is the potential of politicizing infertility as discussions of reproduction take place within scientific and political discourse. Reproductive technology, at one point, opened up a new agenda for women wanting both family and career. It was seen as a progressive move in the women's rights struggle. And yet, the politicization of the practice and the resultant discourse on "property rights" in terms of the female body, and the objectifying of women's bodies as a scientific or political event, may also be seen as regressive. It may be seen as counterproductive, as a woman's body becomes a space of experimentation—a scientific workplace.

The Commercialization of Fertility

Another pressing issue as ART moves into the arena of private industry is the blurring of the distinction between consumer and patient. Certainly, the capitalization of the reproductive technology market raises some concerns. ART is a $3-billion-a-year industry at the intersection of medical practice and private business.

Profit incentives facilitate the process of freezing, storing, and thawing eggs. That eggs have become a commodity is evidenced by the advertisements that blanket college newspapers offering to pay women for egg donations. For consumers, the concern or emphasis of the practice is on product. For patients, there is not only the health and practice concern but also an emotional concern. Skeptics say that a business is not equipped to handle a woman who, despite ART, cannot conceive a child. They question whether a business attitude toward reproduction can answer and identify her needs. Supporters of ART maintain that the right technology, even if driven by economics, offers the best possible means of addressing infertility. On either side of the issue, the word *embryo*, not just as a scientific term but as a business one as well, takes on new connotations.

The process of assisted reproduction can offer only a possibility of a healthy pregnancy, not a guaranteed assurance of conceiving a child and bringing it to term.

Many social implications result from considering fertility as a commercial business; one of these is that fertility becomes a question of affordability. Access to treatment becomes a question of who can pay and who cannot. ART procedures are extremely costly. The fee for freezing eggs can be almost $10,000. The cost of hormone treatments to stimulate egg production can be another $4,000. The future in vitro fertilization of the eggs will cost around $15,000 to $20,000. Critics of the view that technology brings choice point out that financial cost can actually eliminate choice.

For example, infertility rates are much greater outside the United States; yet, because of the high cost, fewer people have access to the technology or treatment. In many countries, infertility comes at the cost of social exclusion, raising questions, again, about the intention of ART to provide an answer to a social need. Even inside the United States, many insurance policies do not provide for ART, excluding families who cannot afford the thousands of dollars the treatments often incur.

In addition, high costs do not necessarily equate to success. The process of assisted reproduction can offer only a possibility of a healthy pregnancy, not a guaranteed assurance of conceiving a child and bringing it to term. Less than half of the procedures performed result in infants carried to term. Critics point out that there is no reimbursement financially or emotionally for undergoing a process that fails in the end. At the same time, proponents maintain that ART practices offer the best possible solution to infertility.

Public dialogue on reproductive technologies is both steeped in controversy and pressingly necessary as our understanding and advancement of the science continues to move forward, creating many medical, ethical, and social questions along the way. Do these technologies oppose traditional family structures? Do lifestyle choices come at the cost of natural, biological practice? What should be the limits of ART as the biological and ethical implications become better understood? Whether for skeptics or for proponents, the advancement of reproductive technology will certainly challenge the intersection of science and society as social and ethical institutions come face to face with medical and scientific exploration.

Prenatal Genetic Screening Enhances Autonomy

Ronald Bailey

Ronald Bailey is a science correspondent at Reason *magazine and author of* Liberation Biology: The Scientific and Moral Case for the Biotech Revolution.

Should prospective parents seek information about gene variants that increase the risk their children will develop diseases as adults? Should physicians provide that information?

Some bioethicists believe that such pre-birth testing is wrong, arguing that the information could stigmatize kids or lead parents to terminate pregnancies of genetically at-risk fetuses. Children, they contend, have a right to an "open future" unburdened by the knowledge of their genetic predispositions for adult onset illnesses.

The Usefulness of Prenatal Genetic Screening

Consider the situation of Amanda and Bradley Kalinsky, as reported on the front page of *The New York Times* in February [2014]. Amanda Kalinsky tested positive for the gene that produces Gerstmann-Straussler-Scheinker (GSS) disease, a form of early onset dementia. Several family members, including her father, had already succumbed to the sickness. When she found out that she was a carrier, she initially vowed never to have children.

But then Amanda and her husband learned that they could use pre-implantation genetic diagnosis of their embryos to avoid passing the GSS gene to their kids. Fertility clinic specialists induced her to produce several eggs that were removed and then fertilized with her husband's sperm. The resulting embryos were tested for the gene, and only those that did not have it were implanted in her womb.

The happy result is that the Kalinskys are the parents of three children—3-year-old twins, Ava and Cole, and 9-month-old Tatum—who have been spared the prospect of suffering the disease that is likely to kill their mother. The cost for the first round of in vitro and testing was about $20,000, which the Kalinskys paid out of pocket. "I would travel that road a million times over if I had to," Amanda told the *Times*, "because in the end I was given the privilege of being their mother."

Researchers can now reveal genetic predispositions ranging from trivial characteristics like eye color and propensity to baldness to the risk of cancer.

In the *Times* article, the Yeshiva University bioethicist David Wasserman argued that discarding the GSS-gene embryos is akin to concluding that people like Amanda Kalinsky should have never been born. But decisions about who should be born ought not to be placed in the hands of ethicists or physicians; they should be left up to the people whose lives and values are actually on the line.

For Kalinsky, the prospect of passing on her GSS gene was frightening enough that she initially ruled out reproducing. Pre-implantation genetic diagnosis enabled her and her husband to have children that they wouldn't have otherwise. In either scenario, the child with the GSS gene was not going to be born; this way, there are three new humans on the planet.

The Advances in Genetic Screening

The Kalinskys were focusing on a single gene. But now a new, much more comprehensive whole-genome screening test is enabling physicians to identify disease risks that parents might not have any reason to suspect, such as genes increasing the possibility of breast cancer or Alzheimer's disease. The new test sequences a fetus's genome based on DNA it sheds into its mother's bloodstream. So researchers can now reveal genetic predispositions ranging from trivial characteristics like eye color and propensity to baldness to the risk of cancer.

Is it ethical for physicians to sequence a fetus's genome and then tell parents what the genetic screening test uncovers? Yes, argues Ignatia B. Van den Veyver of Baylor College in the January 2014 issue of *Prenatal Diagnosis*. Among other arguments, Van den Veyver wonders "whether we infringe autonomy by shielding information that may allow parents and young adults to make decisions about their future that take into consideration all aspects of their current or future health," adding: "It is not well established that not providing this predictive information is the only direction to preserve the right to an open future."

Instead of limiting a child's potential future, knowledge of genetic risks can offer a greater opportunity to inform possibilities for a good life.

Indeed not. Apparently, what some bioethicists mean by "open future" is one in which both parents and children are kept ignorant of the ways their complement of genes may expose them to medical risks.

Prenatal whole-genome sequencing will also provide parents with information about their prospective child's genetic susceptibility to illnesses like lung cancer, arteriosclerosis, and diabetes. Armed with such genomic knowledge, mothers and fathers could make sure that they don't smoke around their kid and later explain why it's a really bad idea for him or her to take up a tobacco habit. Warned in advance about their child's heightened risk of diabetes, parents could devise a diet and exercise regimen aimed at preventing its onset.

Ethical Guidance Based on Autonomy

The American Medical Association (AMA) got it right when it offered ethical guidance to its members on prenatal genetic screening way back in 1994. "If prenatal diagnosis is performed, the principle of patient autonomy requires that all medically relevant information generated from fetal tests be passed along to the parent or parents," the AMA declared. "While the physician should generally discourage requests for information about benign genetic traits, the physician may not ethically refuse to pass along any requested information in his or her possession. The final decision as to what information is deemed appropriate for disclosure can only fall to the parents, informed by the facts and recommendations presented to them by their physician."

More recently, in the January 16 *New England Journal of Medicine*, Ilana Yurkiewicz of Harvard Medical School, Lisa Soleymani Lehmann of Brigham and Women's Hospital, and Bruce Korf of the University of Alabama at Birmingham argue that it is ethical to provide parents with prenatal whole-genome sequencing information, because it is "a basic right of reproductive choice and parental autonomy; people may choose when, with whom, and how to reproduce, and they have the right to data that may inform these decisions." The trio also notes that women in the United States do not have to provide a reason for obtaining an abortion, so it is "difficult to justify restricting abortion in the case of a well-defined reason, such as genetic disease."

The researchers reject the notion that genetic ignorance is somehow liberating. "Instead of limiting a child's potential future, knowledge of genetic risks can offer a greater opportunity to inform possibilities for a good life," they point out.

And that's the essential point. Whatever some bioethicists might believe, autonomy is never enhanced by ignorance.

"Designer Babies" Aren't Coming. The *New York Times* Is Just Trying to Scare You

Jessica Grose

Jessica Grose is a contributor to Slate.

Whenever a new fertility procedure is introduced, some medical ethicists and commentators will conjure up a *Gattaca*-style eugenic future in which all embryos are pre-sorted to look like Uma Thurman and think like Bill Gates. So it goes with a new procedure the Food and Drug Administration [FDA] is considering this week called mitochondrial manipulation technology, which the *New York Times* reported on Tuesday under the headline, "Fear of 'Designer Babies' as FDA Weighs Fertility Procedure." The procedure, which thus far has been performed successfully in monkeys, involves replacing defective mitochondria in one woman's egg with healthy mitochondria from another woman's eggs. Some are referring to this as "three-person embryo fertilization," because, as the *New York Times* writes, it "involves combining the genetic material of three people to make a baby free of certain defects." Sounds great! But apparently there's a significant downside. According to the *Times*, critics fear that the procedure "could lead to the creation of designer babies."

The Opposition to Mitochondrial Manipulation

Opponents of using mitochondrial manipulation in humans, like Marcy Darnovsky, the executive director of the Center for

Genetics and Society, argue that any genetic modification of embryos should be verboten. "Otherwise, we risk venturing into human experimentation and high-tech eugenics," Darnovsky writes in a *New York Times* op-ed. But Nita A. Farahany, a law professor at Duke University and a member of the Presidential Commission for the Study of Bioethical Issues, says that there is a big difference between replacing defective mitochondria and making sure all babies are blue-eyed and blonde.

Some scientists believe that there haven't been enough animal trials to go ahead with the procedure [of mitochondrial manipulation] in humans.

"The majority of the concerns"—like Darnovsky's—"are about opening the flood gates" of genetic manipulation, Farahany told me when we spoke on the phone. They're not really about this specific procedure, she said. That's because the majority of the genome, the traits that are passed on from parent to child, are in the nuclear DNA, not the mitochondrial DNA. This particular procedure only involves mitochondrial DNA. Farahany says that there is a bright line that can be drawn around procedures that involve mitochondria, which create the energy that is necessary for cells to divide.

When a woman's eggs have severe mitochondrial abnormalities, they can have many miscarriages, stillborn children, or extremely sick babies who are unlikely to survive past early childhood. "They will suffer immensely because they can't get the energy" in order for their brains and hearts to grow, says Farahany. They can have extreme pain and difficulty breathing. Fixing this huge amount of suffering for both mother and child seems like a far cry from creating "designer babies," and paramount to any hyped-up concern about a slippery slope.

The Potential for Later Harm

There is, however, a separate set of noneugenic, safety-based concerns about this particular procedure. Some scientists believe that there haven't been enough animal trials to go ahead with the procedure in humans. Others, like Darnovsky, fear that we don't know enough about what happens to subsequent generations after the mitochondrial swap is performed. What if trace abnormalities are left behind, and they don't show up until three generations later?

Still, Farahany believes there is enough data here to proceed to the next step, which would be clinical trials in humans with strong clinical oversight. She points out that other reproductive technologies—like in vitro fertilization, which is now a fairly mainstream procedure—were FDA-approved without knowing what the effect would be on subsequent generations. Farahany also says that in the U.K. [United Kingdom], the HFEA [Human Fertilisation and Embryology Authority], a sort of specialized FDA for reproductive technology, has found that there is broad support for mitochondrial replacement. A separate ethical council in the U.K. has found that it is ethical to proceed.

As for what the FDA (which only looks at the science, not the ethics) will decide, it doesn't look like mitochondrial manipulation technology is going to be approved in the near term. The committee chairman said on Tuesday that many panelists felt "there was probably not enough data in animals . . . to move on to human trials without answering a few additional questions." Farahany says that the FDA is fairly conservative, and she speculated that they wouldn't want to be the first ones to move forward with a controversial procedure like this. She thinks the Brits will probably go first.

"Every time we get a little closer to genetic tinkering to promote health—that's exciting and scary," Dr. Alan Copperman, director of the division of reproductive endocrinology and infertility at Mount Sinai Medical Center in New York, told the *New York Times*. "People are afraid it will turn into a dystopian brave new world." But we're extremely far from a world in which we could—or would want to—manipulate embryos so that they have a variety of "perfect" traits, like our babies were made at the Build-a-Bear workshop. When it comes to this procedure, Farahany has faith that we as a society will build in enough safeguards. "We won't go to the last step, or even to the next step," Farahany says. Once the science is in place for mitochondrial replacement, it seems the suffering that it will alleviate far outweighs the risks.

It's Time to Make Paid Surrogacy Legal in New York

Leslie Morgan Steiner

Leslie Morgan Steiner is author of The Baby Chase: How Surrogacy Is Transforming the American Family.

In 1984, a New Jersey woman named Mary Beth Whitehead agreed to be a surrogate mother for a childless couple, William and Betsy Stern.

Whitehead's own eggs were used and after the girl, Baby M, was born, Whitehead made the emotional decision that she could not give up the baby. She ignored the contract she had signed and refused the $10,000 surrogacy payment.

The New Jersey supreme court invalidated the contract, but the Sterns were still granted full custody of the girl. Whitehead received limited visitation rights.

The case had far-reaching consequences, not the least of which was the outlawing of commercial surrogacy in New York and New Jersey. The only surrogacy allowed in the Empire State is what's known as "compassionate surrogacy," where the woman gestating the baby receives no financial compensation.

But 30 years after Baby M, it's time to reconsider such a sweeping ban—New York should make paid surrogacy legal.

Surrogacy today differs dramatically—medically, morally and legally. Today, most couples and surrogates opt for new-and-improved "gestational surrogacy," where the sperm, egg and uterus come from three separate people. The surrogate becomes pregnant through IVF, and the embryo she gestates is not created from her own egg. She has no biological connection to the baby; legally and genetically, the baby is never her child.

Intended parents, surrogates and lawyers all prefer this surrogacy 2.0, because it clearly delineates the legal parents and grants the surrogate psychological separation from the baby she has helped create. Exploitation of gestational surrogates is rare; surrogates work voluntarily, for a mix of altruistic and financial reasons, and both clients and clinics carefully screen for surrogates who are healthy, mentally grounded and fully aware of the complexity of making someone else's baby dreams come true.

One of the most logical sets of surrogacy regulations, surprisingly, is found in India. Laws there are straightforward and pointedly designed to prevent exploitation of women, destruction of female fetuses and blackmail of clients.

New York could . . . lead the way in regulating paid surrogacy with fair, rational laws that protect donors, surrogates, intended parents and babies.

Only gestational surrogacy is allowed. The intended parents, on the other hand, must have a genetic link to the baby—either through sperm or egg—to avoid a eugenics marketplace where parents seek to engineer a barbaric ideal of physical or genetic superiority.

A surrogate who miscarries cannot work as a surrogate again; there are limits to the number of babies a surrogate can carry and how many times she can be pregnant. Creating a baby via surrogacy is a voluntary, contracted medical procedure with rational rules and guidelines, distinctly different from traditional motherhood.

New York could, like India, lead the way in regulating paid surrogacy with fair, rational laws that protect donors, surrogates, intended parents and babies, backed up by health-insurance coverage that treats infertility as the disease doctors consider it to be.

Making paid surrogacy legal also would make it more affordable. Right now, only the wealthiest New Yorkers can afford the $100,000 or more it costs to pay surrogates in states where the arrangement is legal, such as Connecticut or Maryland.

This is not to trivialize how challenging—morally, legally, financially and psychologically—having a baby via a surrogate can be for everyone involved. Gestational surrogacy's transmogrification of pregnancy and parenthood shakes the human race's centuries-old definition of motherhood.

But we often forget how complicated and emotionally messy parenthood often is, even when achieved the "old-fashioned way." One of the few upsides of infertility—and multifaceted, expensive solutions like surrogacy—is that the disease forces parents and surrogates to confront this complexity of parenthood long before a baby is born.

Infertility is unfair, a cruel, crippling, usually random disease that strikes 10% to 12% of the population without warning. One of the surprises of infertility, for both men and women, is that there is no test for it, so you rarely know you are infertile until you try, and fail, to conceive a baby.

It is made even more unfair when the state outlaws one of your options. Surrogacy should be made legal because hopeful parents, dedicated doctors and empathetic surrogates all believe in one simple truth: that everyone who wants a baby should be able to have a baby.

Gattaca at 15: The Dystopian Sci-Fi Thriller Is Fast Becoming Our Reality

Daniel Allott

Daniel Allott is a writer in Washington, DC.

In a key scene in the film *Gattaca*, a genetic counselor speaks with a young couple about the child they'd like to have. The couple's first child, Vincent, was diagnosed immediately after birth with several disabilities including a heart defect that puts his life expectancy at just 30.2 years.

So the couple decide to genetically engineer their second child. The counselor explains that after screening hundreds of embryos produced via in vitro fertilization, they are left with two healthy boy embryos and two healthy girl embryos. "All that remains is to select the most compatible candidate," he tells them.

They decide they want another boy, a playmate for Vincent. Reading off a report, the counselor says, "You have specified hazel eyes, dark hair and fair skin." (The counselor, who is black, smiles a little as he reads the last specification.)

He continues, "I have taken the liberty of eradicating any potentially prejudicial conditions: premature baldness, myopia, alcoholism, addictive susceptibility, propensity for violence, obesity, etc."

The mother interjects, "We didn't want ... I mean, diseases, yes, but. . . ."

Her husband says, "Right, we were just wondering if it's good just to leave a few things to chance."

The geneticist says, "You want to give your child the best possible start."

Believe me we have enough imperfection built in already. Your child doesn't need any additional burdens. Keep in mind this child is still you, only the best of you. You could conceive a thousand times and never get such a result.

The couple acquiesces, and their second son, Anton, is the near genetically perfect son they had hoped for—their one-in-a-thousand baby.

Fifteen years after the film's release, advances in reproductive and genetic medicine are producing the type of society Gattaca *warned against.*

In *Gattaca*'s world, most parents genetically engineer their children, and the few parents who conceive naturally risk producing children who become members of an underclass called "invalids."

Set in the "not too distant future," *Gattaca*, which starred Ethan Hawke, Uma Thurman, and Jude Law, debuted on October 24, 1997. The dystopian sci-fi thriller is a cautionary tale of what could happen if humanity doesn't check its eugenic impulses.

Fifteen years after the film's release, advances in reproductive and genetic medicine are producing the type of society *Gattaca* warned against.

The fields of assisted reproduction and genetics have been transformed since 1997. The Human Genome Project was completed in 2003, which enhanced our understanding of the genetic roots of human traits.

It took ten years and more than $3 billion to sequence the first human genome (DNA). But some scientists believe it won't be long before a person's full genetic make-up could be decoded in hours and for less than $1,000.

Even now couples can discern a great deal about their children before they are born. Genetic testing is being mainstreamed into the practice of obstetrics. In 2007, the American College of Obstetricians and Gynecologists began recommending that all women be offered prenatal screening for genetic conditions.

Many doctors encourage pregnant women to obtain prenatal genetic screening, and, if the test comes back positive for a genetic condition, to abort. A recent survey found that a quarter of physicians admitted trying to influence mothers' decisions, usually encouraging them to end the life of a genetically disadvantaged child.

New DNA testing can screen fetuses for hundreds of genetic traits in the first trimester of pregnancy. Such tests are becoming cheaper, less invasive and more widely available. One test uses tiny amounts of free-floating DNA in the mother's blood stream that can give researchers a baby's entire genetic code.

In June researchers at the University of Washington announced a new technique that can map a fetus's DNA and thus make it easier to prenatally alter the genetic makeup of a developing child. Researchers say such a procedure may be available in clinics in as little as five years.

Some experts believe this new technology is changing parents' attitudes toward their children.

Pre-implantation genetic diagnosis (PGD) continues to grow in popularity. PGD allows parents to create designer babies. First, embryos are created via IVF; then, after a few days of growth in a lab, the embryos are screened, and those that are determined to have higher risk of having certain traits, including genetic disabilities or the "wrong" sex, are killed. (PGD is a favorite among Indian and Chinese nationals, who travel to the U.S. for the procedure because their own countries outlaw the practice.) Embryos who pass the screening process are transferred to the mother's womb to continue developing.

A 2006 study by Johns Hopkins University found that 42 percent of fertility clinics offered PGD for sex selection. Dr. Jeffrey Steinberg of The Fertility Institutes uses PGD and has suggested that he will be able to screen embryos for eye and hair color within a few years.

Some experts believe this new technology is changing parents' attitudes toward their children. President Bush's Council on Bioethics warned in 2003, "The attitude of parents toward their child may be quietly shifting from unconditional acceptance to critical scrutiny: the very first act of parenting now becomes not the unreserved welcoming of an arriving child, but the judging of his or her fitness, while still an embryo, to become their child, all by the standards of contemporary genetic screening."

A 2009 poll reported in the *Journal of Genetic Counseling* found that a majority of respondents would elect to have prenatal genetic testing for mental retardation (75 percent) and deafness (54 percent). Thirteen percent even said they'd desire testing for superior intelligence. The authors concluded: "Our study suggests that consumers desire more reproductive genetic testing than what is currently offered; however, their selection of tests suggests self-imposed limits on testing."

In an interview, Arthur Caplan, head of the Division of Bioethics at New York University Langone Medical Center, predicted that within a decade, prenatal genetic screening will be available not only for physical and mental traits but also for behavioral conditions such as schizophrenia, depression, proneness to addiction, and even sexual orientation.

"We may all think that parents and society are very interested in diseases," he told me, "but I'm here to say that they're also very interested in personality and behavior."

Many parents feel they have a right to genetically perfect children, and courts are increasingly willing to recognize that right. At least 28 states recognize "wrongful birth" lawsuits, in which parents of disabled children are granted compensation when doctors fail to inform them that their unborn child may be at higher risk of a genetic disorder.

Soon it will be a sin for parents to have a child that carries the heavy burden of genetic disease.

Caplan believes American culture reinforces parents' desire for genetic perfection. He said:

> There's going to be demand in a society oriented toward do-ing well, toward perfection, toward the value of the best you can be, even a society that says, "I want a better life for my child than I had for myself." That's an ethical principle that you can hear in every religion, you can hear it in secular society—it's just around. So somebody's going to say "Why won't I test my kids, to [give] them a better life than I had?"

Given all these changes, how long will it be before mothers feel obligated either to abort "imperfect" babies or to manipu-late the genes of their embryo-children?

How long until those who do not get tested will be re-garded as immoral? As Robert Edwards—test tube baby pio-neer and Nobel Prize winner—has said, "Soon it will be a sin for parents to have a child that carries the heavy burden of genetic disease."

Caplan explained where this view might lead:

> Down the road, disability is likely to have more stigma, be-cause people will ask this question: "Why did you choose to have a kid with a disability if you could have tested and avoided that? It's your fault." At some point the government might come along and say "It's so expensive to have disabil-ity, here's our policy: You can't make a baby unless you have

genetic testing. That is to say, we think it's a cost containment feature in the year 2030 for everyone to have genetic testing."

If you don't think that's going to happen here, start looking at what genetic testing looks like in Singapore, start thinking about what genetic testing looks like in China. Start thinking about cultures where people are saying, "Hey, we'd like to build better babies. It'll make us more competitive. We've had a one-baby rule. Now we're going to have a mandatory genetic testing rule."

Philosopher Jeremy Rifkin predicts the formation of an "informal genetic caste system," which harkens to *Gattaca*, a world where "a minute drop of blood determines where you can work, who you should marry, what you're capable of achieving." Indeed as an "invalid," Vincent must work as a janitor and can only fantasize about becoming an astronaut.

Some bioethicists make the moral case for genetic enhancements. Ethicists like Peter Singer have called for government subsidies to parents to "genetically improve their offspring." In his 2010 book *Enhancing Evolution: The Ethical Case for Making Better People*, John Harris argues that genetic enhancement is not only morally defensible but morally obligatory.

A fundamental misconception at the root of the Gattaca *mindset is that persons with disabilities inevitably lead unhappy lives.*

Bioethicist Julian Savulescu agrees and has developed a philosophy called "procreative beneficence." He argues that "Parents should use technology to manipulate their children's memory, temperament, patience, empathy, sense of humor, optimism and other characteristics in order to give them the best opportunity of the best life."

The use of genetic technology raises many questions. Most of us are troubled by the idea of "playing God." Many people believe that children are gifts to be appreciated as they come to us, not as instruments of our ambition or as objects to be manufactured and commoditized.

A fundamental misconception at the root of the *Gattaca* mindset is that persons with disabilities inevitably lead unhappy lives and overburden their families and society.

But that's demonstrably untrue. To take just one example, a 2011 survey found that 99 percent of adults with Down syndrome report being happy with their lives. Another study found that 79 percent of parents of people with Down syndrome reported their outlook on life was more positive because of their child. Also, 97 percent of siblings of people with DS expressed feelings of pride and 88 percent were convinced they were better people because of their sibling with DS.

In *Gattaca*, Vincent assumes the identity of Jerome, a former swimming star with a near perfect genetic profile who was injured in a car accident that left him paralyzed from the waist down. Vincent pays Jerome for his identity, using his valid DNA in blood, hair, tissue, and urine samples to pass the constant screenings as he attempts to become an astronaut (which he ultimately does).

But Jerome feels marginalized in a society obsessed with perfection. He becomes an alcoholic and ends up killing himself by climbing inside his home incinerator and lighting a fire.

The eugenic mentality behind *Gattaca* fails to appreciate the value of human difference. *Gattaca* tries to eradicate human weakness but can't because weakness and disability are natural and essential parts of the human experience. They are part of what it means to be human.

Whenever I re-watch *Gattaca*, and as I observe the quickly developing culture of genetic perfection around me, I think about questions posed by Melinda Tankard Reist in her book

Defiant Birth. Her simple questions get to the heart of what's wrong with the *Gattaca* mentality.

She asks: "Who is disabled? The person who through no fault of his own lives a more difficult life? Or is it the society which cannot tolerate or accept this person among them?"

Three-Parent Embryos Illustrate Ethical Problems with Technologies

Brendan P. Foht

Brendan P. Foht is assistant editor at New Atlantis: A Journal of Technology and Society.

The decision by the British government earlier this summer [2013] to approve a suite of new technologies that would make possible the creation of human embryos with three genetic parents has brought a long-simmering and seemingly obscure bioethical debate into the public eye, raising questions not only about the future of human reproductive technologies but also about some practices that have been with us for decades.

The British decision followed recommendations from the country's Human Fertilisation and Embryology Authority in March of this year and a major bioethics report cautiously endorsing the techniques last year. The debate has muddied the lines between left and right. Liberal groups like the Center for Genetics and Society strongly oppose the new technologies, while some liberal bioethicists like Arthur Caplan have said the new techniques are "worth the ethical risk." Conservative bioethics commentator Wesley J. Smith, a frequent contributor to these pages, has argued that the new technologies are unethical, while the editors of *Real Clear Science*, who are scourges of the "antiscientific left," have endorsed the new technologies.

The Destruction of Embryos

The techniques in question involve transplanting the chromosomes from a single-cell embryo or from an unfertilized egg into a donor egg or embryo from which the chromosomes have been removed. These procedures were developed with a therapeutic intention: They would allow women with mitochondrial disorders to have children who will not inherit those disorders. (Mutations in the mitochondrial DNA can cause a host of serious illnesses.) Unlike in egg or embryo donation, which are methods widely used at in vitro fertilization clinics and would prevent the transmission of these disorders, the children created through the new techniques would be genetically related to the women undergoing the procedure, having inherited her nuclear DNA but not her mitochondrial DNA. What has been most controversial about these techniques is that they would create embryos with *three* genetic parents: The embryos would inherit chromosomes from one mother and one father, but would also inherit mitochondrial DNA (which contains a small number of additional genes) from the donated embryo or egg cell.

Countless human embryos are destroyed on a regular basis as a result of the way IVF is practiced in the United States today.

Before focusing on the three-parent issue, let us first look at other objections that have been raised. As Alex Berezow of *Real Clear Science* notes, some critics "worry about the ethics of destroying embryos," since one of the new techniques involves the destruction of embryos. But he dismisses this concern by pointing out that "standard IVF also destroys embryos," which is, unfortunately, all too often true, though this new way of making babies would destroy embryos in a different way from the usual practice of IVF.

The new embryo-destructive technique, known as "pronu-clear transfer," involves an early-stage embryo—one in which the chromosomes from the egg and sperm have not yet joined together in a single nucleus. The pronuclei are extracted, de-stroying that embryo. The extracted genetic material is then transferred into another, similarly enucleated (and thus destroyed) embryo, but one that was created using a donated egg, thereby creating a new embryo that contains the chromo-somes of the man and woman who intend to become parents, as well as the mitochondrial DNA of the egg donor. The de-struction of embryos in ordinary IVF results from the dis-carding of "excess" embryos, or of embryos deemed geneti-cally defective following screening tests. This new technique would be the first assisted-reproductive technology involving the deliberate destruction of human embryos as a necessary part of the procedure.

Berezow is of course correct that countless human em-bryos are destroyed on a regular basis as a result of the way IVF is practiced in the United States today. That might also lead us to ask whether we have been right to tolerate the cava-lier destruction of embryos as just part of the way the U.S. IVF industry does business. Indeed, ordinary IVF *could* be practiced in a way that would not result in the destruction of human embryos; in Germany, for instance, it is illegal to cre-ate "excess" embryos during IVF treatments.

The Children Created by Genetic Engineering

Another objection to these new techniques relates to the risks they will pose to the created children. While there have been a few preliminary studies, the risks are still poorly understood. Against these critics, Berezow writes that "a mother with a mito-chondrial disease who wishes to have her own children may very well choose to accept the risk." Indeed she may, but the child born through this experimental procedure is obviously in no position to accept the risk.

There is one other frequently raised objection to these technologies that seems misguided, namely, that they are a form of "genetic engineering" or, as bioethicist Margaret Somerville put it in a column for the *Ottawa Citizen*, that they would be a form of *inheritable* genetic engineering. Children who are created using these methods would pass their modified genes on to their children. Rather than worrying about whether using a new technology might give future generations different genetic characteristics than they would otherwise have inherited, we should be concerned about the way genetic engineering can alter the *relationship between the generations* from one of parents accepting the novelty and spontaneous uniqueness of their children to one where parents use biotechnology to choose and control the biological nature of their children.

The prospect of genetic engineering that these new ways of manipulating embryos and their DNA raise helps us to see what is morally problematic in the existing technologies.

That said, it is far from clear that these new techniques enable such morally problematic technological mastery. In a debate held earlier this year on whether genetic engineering should be prohibited, Duke law professor Nita Farahany argued that these new techniques will not lead "to a dystopia of designing perfect babies," emphasizing that they would simply prevent the transmission of various disease-causing genes to give parents healthy children. The aim of giving parents babies that are genetically related to them but free of debilitating heritable diseases is perfectly understandable, and not one that should be confused with the morally twisted aims of eugenics or of the specter of "designer babies."

Ironically, Farahany's opponents in the debate, who argued that genetic engineering should be prohibited, pointed to pre-implantation genetic diagnosis (PGD) as a morally acceptable alternative. PGD allows doctors and parents to test embryos prior to implanting them, allowing them to select those with the "best" genes. For the most part, PGD aims simply to give parents children who are healthy, rather than perfectly designed. But PGD can also be used to select for any number of genetic traits, and is often used to select the sex of the embryo, a clear case of using technology to control important biological characteristics of the next generation.

And even beyond technologies like PGD, some forms of genetic control are already exercised through existing reproductive technologies and practices, such as finding and paying young women with high SAT scores for their eggs. But the fact that our society already engages in forms of genetic control that are arguably more serious and problematic than what these new procedures would offer does not, of course, justify embarking on these experimental reproductive technologies. Rather, the prospect of genetic engineering that these new ways of manipulating embryos and their DNA raise helps us to see what is morally problematic in the existing technologies.

The Creation of Three-Parent Embryos

Let's return to the most shocking aspect of these techniques, the fact that they create children with three parents. Defenders may say we already do something similar with egg and embryo donation or in surrogacy arrangements. In these cases, the child has a genetic mother and a genetic father but also a *gestational* mother, who carries the child to term but is not genetically related. But even though gestation is not a form of genetic parenthood, it is hard to deny that being pregnant for nine months creates an important biological, not to say emotional and personal, tie with the child.

Again, it would seem that we have come to accept arrangements that split apart the various biological and social aspects of parenthood, and that deliberately create families where children will never know one or both of their genetic parents. But do these practices justify carving up parenthood into even finer parts with these new methods that create three-parent embryos?

Perhaps the disquiet we feel when we hear about the creation of embryos with three parents should lead us to reconsider whether these other technological distortions were morally justifiable in the first place. Evidence collected in a 2010 report from the Institute for American Values suggests that donor-conceived children may experience serious emotional suffering as a result of the circumstances of their conception and the confusion surrounding their identity.

A common rhetorical strategy for defending controversial new biotechnologies is to point out that there are plenty of things we already do that are morally problematic and to argue that, for the sake of consistency, we should accept the new technology as well. Consistency is obviously important, but we should strive to be consistently good, not consistently base, and we should not assume that our horror at something new is ill-founded simply because we realize that what we find horrible is already all around us.

The repugnance that we feel when we contemplate new biotechnologies that violate the natural order of the family may indeed be, as Leon Kass famously argued, a source of deep wisdom that can help guide us through the possibilities that the future has in store. As we consider the mixed blessings of the biotechnology project that society has already grown to accept, we should reflect on how our reactions to what seems shocking and new can bring renewed clarity to the moral meaning of what has become all too familiar.

Breeding Exploitation:
The Faces of Surrogacy

Jennifer Lahl, interviewed by Kathryn Jean Lopez

Jennifer Lahl is founder and president of The Center for Bioethics and Culture Network, and Kathryn Jean Lopez is editor-at-large of National Review Online.

Jennifer Lahl brings her nursing expertise to the conversation about surrogacy with her new documentary, *Breeders*, a project of the Center for Bioethics and Culture Network. *Breeders* opens a window into surrogacy and its devaluing and demeaning of women and life, showing the details of an industry in which realities are often masked by unobjectionable words like "hope," assuming the best of intentions and practices. In an interview with *National Review Online*'s Kathryn Jean Lopez, Lahl talks about *Breeders*, surrogacy, and her hopes for the future of reproduction technology. (Full disclosure: Lopez has endorsed the documentary.)

Kathryn Jean Lopez: Why Breeders now?

Jennifer Lahl: Much of my work is in the space of reproductive technologies, and specifically what is called third-party reproduction (using eggs, sperm, or wombs of other people to have a baby). *Breeders* is the third and final film in this series. First was *Eggsploitation*, which looked at the lives and stories of women who sold their eggs for much needed money, and who suffered serious health complications as a result. Then we released *Anonymous Father's Day*, telling the stories of adults created via anonymous sperm donation. We felt it was important to tell the whole story of third-party reproduction, which compelled us to tell the surrogacy story in *Breeders*.

Lopez: Who is your audience?

Lahl: Our primary audience is the young-adult crowd—those most heavily recruited and targeted to sell their eggs or sperm or rent out their wombs as a means of helping others while earning money.

Lopez: Isn't surrogacy about hope and any criticism about it insensitive to infertility?

We're moving away from the traditional method of surrogacy, where the surrogate is both the birth mother and the genetic mother ..., to what is referred to as gestational surrogacy.

Lahl: Well, that is certainly how the supporters of surrogacy feel about it. There is a case now in Utah where a 58-year-old woman is the surrogate for her daughter, basically giving birth to her own grandchild. The comments on this case are mostly about the miracle and the amazing thing this woman is doing for her daughter. It is often the case that those like me, who are critical of the practice, are seen as insensitive and lacking compassion for those struggling to carry a child to term. I am very sympathetic to those struggling with infertility; it is tremendously painful. But we would be remiss if we only looked at the issue from the perspective of those who want a baby. What about the needs and concerns of the child? What about the use of women—very often women who are of low income—as surrogates, which some refer to as incubators, breeders, and even Easy-Bake Ovens? What about the commercialization and commodification aspects of what is now a multi-billion-dollar-per-year fertility industry? Much of my work is trying to tell the full story, the whole story, which requires that we face these questions and not avoid them because someone so desperately wants a baby.

Lopez: What's the important connection to Eggsploitation? (And what does it mean to eggsploit?)

Lahl: It is often the case in surrogacy that "donor" eggs are used. There has been a shift in surrogacy. We're moving away from the traditional method of surrogacy, where the surrogate is both the birth mother and the genetic mother (think Baby M case), to what is referred to as gestational surrogacy, meaning the surrogate supplies her womb but the egg comes either from the intended mother or from a "donor." Male same-sex couples need both an egg donor and a surrogate in order to have a child. The shift toward gestational surrogacy is a deliberate move made for legal reasons. The less a woman can claim a link to the child (i.e., a genetic link), the less intended parents worry that the surrogate will be allowed to change her mind.

Yes, it is hard work. I've been surprised just how hard it is because the emotions are so real, so deep, and . . . everyone either has used or knows someone who has used these technologies to conceive.

In addition, intended parents may feel they have a stronger legal case against a surrogate if she should change her mind about giving up a child to which she has no genetic connection. Of course, who then is looking out for the child? In particular, what is the impact of being in the womb for nine months and immediately being separated from the only person that the baby has ever known? We've learned from adoption history that babies know their birth mothers, and that both mothers and babies experience a loss from such separation.

To eggsploit means to literally use women for their eggs. Egg "donation" (in reality, egg selling) has serious, real, short- and long-term health risks. It is scandalous that we allow young women to be paid to undergo a risky procedure, corrupting their health decisions with a check for $5,000, $10,000, or more. When people watch *Eggsploitation*, I'm overwhelmed with how many in the audience are woefully uninformed about this practice and how many are alarmed when they discover that it is legal.

Lopez: What are the fundamental questions we need to ask about assisted reproduction? Who should be asking and how?

Lahl: Should we be doing this at all? seems a fundamental question in my mind. Do we have a right, a fundamental right, to have a child? What limits should be in place for people using these new technologies to have a child? These are questions we all should be addressing. As a nurse, I'm disappointed the medical professionals aren't encouraging this conversation. And our lawmakers must see these as important and serious questions to be wrestling with. As it is now, these messy cases get caught up in our courts in order to decide who gets the baby, or who the rightful or legal parent is.

Lopez: It's hard to ask these questions, isn't it, when so many Americans seem to have made use of some kind of assisted reproduction? If you're in a classroom teaching, how many students could be products of these technologies?

Lahl: Yes, it is hard work. I've been surprised just how hard it is because the emotions are so real, so deep, and yes, everyone either has used or knows someone who has used these technologies to conceive. Often when I speak to a large audience I will say that I know many in the room have used these technologies, are here because of these technologies, or may be here because of these technologies but don't even know it (many people don't tell their children they were born via donated eggs or sperm).

Lopez: Hasn't this all gone too far for it to be possible to roll anything back?

Lahl: We have a history, at least here in the U.S., of making large-scale changes in thinking and behavior. Smoking is a good example of a product that was rolled back because we became aware of the risks and harms. Seatbelts in cars is another example of a large-scale change. I'm old enough to remember standing up in the backseat of the car when my family went somewhere. My hope is that as we are now increasingly seeing the fallout and the negative consequences for both women and children, we will begin regulating these technologies like many other countries have done.

Lopez: How much does gay marriage factor into the questions Breeders raises?

Lahl: The majority of people using surrogates are heterosexual couples, but with the growing acceptance of same-sex relationships, homosexual couples too are seeing this as a way to have a child of their own.

Lopez: How important is the maternal-bonding question to surrogacy?

Lahl: I was a pediatric nurse for nearly 20 years, and the bonding issue is a real concern of mine. As a nurse I worked mostly in the intensive care unit, and we worked so hard to keep moms with sick preemie babies connected and attached because that bond is so important. We are learning more and more about all the important things that happen those nine months in the womb, but in surrogacy we simply ignore the importance of maternal-child bonding, treating it as irrelevant because someone who desperately wants a baby gets one.

I never watched someone give truly informed consent to medical risks while staring at a check for $20,000–$30,000, which is what a surrogate can easily make.

Lopez: Should there be any exceptions? Are there conditions in which surrogacy is a merciful option, like if a sister wants to help a brother and sister-in-law, etc.?

Lahl: Again, although I have compassion on those who can't carry a child to term, I don't think the ends justify the means. We can't predict how these situations will end up. One of the women we interview in *Breeders* was a surrogate for her brother, and that went terribly wrong. I'm in the process of interviewing an egg donor now who has just been diagnosed with cancer. A surrogate I know lives with daily regret knowing the child she surrendered is in a less than loving home. The Baby M case is the classic case of a woman who changed her mind and couldn't surrender the baby. I want to build a society where we want mothers to connect with their babies and not turn their bodies into objects to be used, bought, or sold.

Lopez: What's the unique voice you bring to this as a nurse?

Lahl: My expertise is unique because I can speak to the real risks and harms of the drugs and procedures used on women. I understand the medical problems that children have who are conceived through reproductive technologies. Many seem to think this is all so easy and that a woman just donates eggs, loans out her uterus, and a baby almost miraculously appears (as if carried in by a stork). As a pediatric nurse, I have expertise in maternal-child health. And I understand the use of and corruption of informed consent. In my 20-something years of nursing, I never watched someone give truly informed consent to medical risks while staring at a check for $20,000–$30,000, which is what a surrogate can easily make.

Lopez: What Breeders story is most compelling to you? Whose testimony do you wish everyone would listen to?

Lahl: That's a hard question. Maybe it's because I'm a female documentary filmmaker, but I just fall in love with all of the people I interview in my films. Their stories, bravely told, are each so very compelling. They all started out wanting to really help someone, but things went so terribly wrong. Heather is so vulnerable as she talks about being told to abort the baby she was carrying but refusing. Tanya, who closes the film—when the cameras were rolling and she was telling her story, I just knew we had the ending to the film! Cindy's case is gut-wrenching, as she was truly used by a man to have babies for himself and his partner. Gail, who was the surrogate for her brother and his partner, has an important story, since people think surrogacy within families is the best or only way to go. Her case demonstrates that even then everything can go terribly wrong.

Lopez: Is this a women's-rights issue? A health issue? A human-rights issue?

I believe our best contribution is educating ordinary people so that they will think twice about these practices.

Lahl: Yes, yes, and yes! It is a women's-rights issue, which is why I've been able to get such support for my work from a diverse range of leading international feminists. It is definitely a health issue: the risks of the technologies, the drugs, and the separation to both the women and the children. And it's a human-rights issue, especially when you see how poor women in India, Thailand, or Mexico are treated. Often these are illiterate women who can't even read the contracts they're agreeing to. They are truly impoverished and simply cannot be making free and informed choices in such circumstances.

Lopez: As a political issue: What's next and realistic to do?

Lahl: Part of our educational work is directed toward lawmakers. Last year we saw legislative successes in Minnesota on a surrogacy bill. We were influential in Louisiana, where Governor Bobby Jindal vetoed a surrogacy bill. Governor Jerry Brown vetoed a bill that would have allowed researchers to pay women for eggs in my state of California. We are watching a bill in the District of Columbia that would make surrogacy legal there. These aren't issues that politicians gravitate toward, though. No one makes third-party reproduction one of their platform goals.

But I believe our best contribution is educating ordinary people so that they will think twice about these practices. I've met several young women who were thinking about selling their eggs but watched *Eggsploitation* and it changed their minds. I hope *Breeders* will have the same impact.

Lopez: What does a parent say to a child who was conceived through exploitation of a poor woman?

Lahl: Honesty is still the best policy. I'm a believer in telling your children as early as they can understand how they were conceived. Acknowledge and accept their feelings of loss, grief, or anger. I've learned a lot from my friends who were conceived through anonymous sperm donation and also the young woman in *Breeders* born via surrogacy. They really are truly happy to be alive, but they want (and are right to want) and need validation of their real feelings.

Unethical Uses of Reproductive Technologies

Margaret Somerville

Margaret Somerville is professor of faculty medicine, the Samuel Gale Professor of Law, and the founding director of the Centre for Medicine, Ethics, and Law at McGill University.

A few days ago, I was asked what I thought about Kristine Casey, a 61-year-old woman giving birth to her grandson. Ms. Casey had acted as a surrogate mother for the child of her daughter and son-in-law.

My gut reaction was that this was ethically wrong. But was that reaction correct and could it be justified?

The Ethics of Human Reproduction

We must first ask is surrogate motherhood, in general, ethically acceptable? I don't believe it is for a wide variety of reasons, including that it breaches children's human rights regarding their coming-into-being; it exploits poor women; and its international commercialization has opened up dehumanizing scenarios, such as FedEx-ing frozen embryos to "warehouses" of surrogates in developing countries.

But, as is so often true in trying to decide on the ethics of human reproduction, especially regarding reproductive technologies, there is no consensus. And I know from experience that, faced with a sobbing woman unable to carry her and her husband's child, who is distraught that payment of surrogate mothers has been prohibited and says, "I can't believe you would disagree with our doing anything we can to have our child," it's very difficult to say, "No, I don't agree with you hiring a surrogate mother."

For the sake of exploring the issues, let's assume some surrogacy will continue to be allowed. What restrictions are ethically required?

Our choice of words can affect our assessment of the ethics, probably because they influence our emotions and intuitions, which are validly taken into account in making ethical decisions. Grandmother Casey is compellingly described as "altruistic" and "giving the ultimate gift" to her daughter and her son-in-law.

But let's change the situation slightly and see if we make the same assessment of ethical acceptability.

Questions About Unethical Family Structures

A young infertile man and his wife want to have a baby that is as closely genetically related to them and their family as possible, including because in their culture blood relationship is considered very important.

> We must start from a basic presumption that the child's rights to be born into a natural family structure in which the family relationships have not been intentionally confused, must be given priority.

The man's father wants to donate sperm to artificially inseminate his daughter-in-law. The child will be the half-brother of his social father, and the biological child of his social grandfather. Is this ethically acceptable?

If not, but the surrogate grandmother is seen as ethically acceptable, is it because she was not the biological mother? Would it be acceptable to inseminate a still fertile woman with the sperm of her infertile daughter's husband? And what about a woman donating ova to her daughter, which results in a child of the daughter's husband and his mother-in-law?

Does it make a difference if we change the generational relationships and a sperm donor was the infertile husband's brother, not his father? Likewise, what about a sister donating ova to her sister, or, as is not uncommon, a sister carrying a baby for her sister? Is the latter less ethically worrisome than a grandmother doing so and, if so, why?

I believe that we must start from a basic presumption that the child's rights to be born into a natural family structure in which the family relationships have not been intentionally confused, must be given priority. If surrogacy, in general, or any particular instance of surrogacy is not in a child's "best interests" in such regards, it is unethical. The same "child's best interests principle" should apply to all uses of reproductive technologies.

The Confusion of Family

Sometimes a distinction between repairing nature when it fails and doing something that would never happen in nature can be helpful in looking at ethics. A grandmother giving birth to her biological grandchild is something that could never happen in nature, and so I'd say no to such surrogacy arrangements.

A woman giving birth to her own child conceived with her son-in-law, even though it's not incest (there is no sexual intercourse and no blood relationship between them, as the crime of incest requires), is, I believe, ethically reprehensible. Likewise, inseminating a woman with her father-in-law's sperm.

If for no other reason, the confusion of family structures and roles that these possibilities would cause make them unethical. Some might see them as the free choice of the adults involved and, therefore, ethically acceptable. But the child, the most vulnerable person, which is ethically relevant, and the one most likely to be harmfully affected, has made no such choice and given no consent.

One response to this argument is that the child has no right to complain, as he or she wouldn't exist except for the steps undertaken. Joanna Rose, a donor-conceived adult who objects to donor conception, responded, "If I were the product of rape, I would still be glad to be alive, but that doesn't mean I or anyone else should approve of rape or that it's ethical."

The bottom line, regarding surrogate motherhood, and all uses of reproductive technologies, should be that when adults' claims to use these technologies clash with the rights or "best interests" of the resulting children, the latter must prevail. So far, our decisions have been mainly based on the opposite priority. If we examine past decisions using this new basis, in some cases we might change our minds about what is and is not ethical.

CHAPTER 4

Is It Ethical for Medical Professionals to End Life?

Overview: Views on End-of-Life Medical Treatments

Pew Research Center

The Pew Research Center is a nonpartisan fact tank that informs the public about the issues, attitudes, and trends shaping America and the world.

At a time of national debate over health care costs and insurance, a Pew Research Center survey on end-of-life decisions finds most Americans say there are some circumstances in which doctors and nurses should allow a patient to die. At the same time, however, a growing minority says that medical professionals should do everything possible to save a patient's life *in all circumstances*.

Views on End-of-Life Medical Treatment

When asked about end-of-life decisions for other people, two-thirds of Americans (66%) say there are at least some situations in which a patient should be allowed to die, while nearly a third (31%) say that medical professionals always should do everything possible to save a patient's life. Over the last quarter-century, the balance of opinion has moved modestly away from the majority position on this issue. While still a minority, the share of the public that says doctors and nurses should do everything possible to save a patient's life has gone up 9 percentage points since 2005 and 16 points since 1990.

The uptick comes partly from a modest decline in the share that says there are circumstances in which a patient should be allowed to die and partly from an increase in the

Pew Research Center, "Views on End-of-Life Medical Treatments," November 2013, pp. 5–11. http://www.pewforum.org/2013/11/21/views-on-end-of-life-medical-treatments. All rights reserved. Reproduced with permission.

share of the public that expresses an opinion; the portion that has no opinion or declines to answer the survey question went down from 12% in 1990 to 8% in 2005 and now stands at 3%.

When thinking about a more personal situation, many Americans express preferences for end-of-life medical treatment that vary depending on the exact circumstances they might face. A majority of adults say there are at least some situations in which they, personally, would want to halt medical treatment and be allowed to die. For example, 57% say they would tell their doctors to stop treatment if they had a disease with no hope of improvement and were suffering a great deal of pain. And about half (52%) say they would ask their doctors to stop treatment if they had an incurable disease and were totally dependent on someone else for their care. But about a third of adults (35%) say they would tell their doctors to do everything possible to keep them alive—even in dire circumstances, such as having a disease with no hope of improvement and experiencing a great deal of pain. In 1990, by comparison, 28% expressed this view. This modest uptick stems largely from an increase in the share of the public that expresses a preference on these questions; the share saying they would stop their treatments so they could die has remained about the same over the past 23 years.

Personal preferences about end-of-life treatment are strongly related to religious affiliation as well as race and ethnicity.

At the same time, a growing share of Americans also believe individuals have a moral right to end their own lives. About six-in-ten adults (62%) say that a person suffering a great deal of pain with no hope of improvement has a moral right to commit suicide, up from 55% in 1990. A 56% majority also says this about those who have an incurable disease, up from 49% in 1990. While far fewer (38%) believe there is a moral right to suicide when someone is "ready to die because living has become a burden," the share saying this is up 11 percentage points, from 27% in 1990. About a third of adults (32%) say a person has a moral right to suicide when he or she "is an extremely heavy burden on his or her family," roughly the same share as in 1990 (29%).

Meanwhile, the public remains closely divided on the issue of physician-assisted suicide: 47% approve and 49% disapprove of laws that would allow a physician to prescribe lethal doses of drugs that a terminally ill patient could use to commit suicide. Attitudes on physician-assisted suicide were roughly the same in 2005 (when 46% approved and 45% disapproved).

Religion and End-of-Life Care

Personal preferences about end-of-life treatment are strongly related to religious affiliation as well as race and ethnicity. For example, most white mainline Protestants (72%), white Catholics (65%) and white evangelical Protestants (62%) say they would stop their medical treatment if they had an incurable disease and were suffering a great deal of pain. By contrast, most black Protestants (61%) and 57% of Hispanic Catholics say they would tell their doctors to do everything possible to save their lives in the same circumstances. On balance, blacks and Hispanics are less likely than whites to say they would halt medical treatment if they faced these kinds of situations.

Religious groups also differ strongly in their beliefs about the morality of suicide. About half of white evangelical Protestants and black Protestants reject the idea that a person has a moral right to suicide in all four circumstances described in the survey. By comparison, the religiously unaffiliated, white mainline Protestants and white Catholics are more likely to say there *is* a moral right to commit suicide in each of the four situations considered. There is a similar pattern among religious groups when it comes to allowing physician-assisted suicide for the terminally ill.

These are some of the key findings from the Pew Research Center telephone survey, which was conducted on landlines and cellphones from March 21 to April 8, 2013, among a nationally representative sample of 1,994 adults. The margin of error for the survey is plus or minus 2.9 percentage points. . . .

There has been only modest change over time in the level of public attention to, and preparation for, end-of-life medical decisions.

Preparing for End-of-Life Decisions

The share of the total U.S. population that is age 65 and older has more than tripled over the last century, from roughly 4% in 1900 to 14% in 2012. But despite the graying of America, a sizable minority of the populace has not thought about the kinds of medical decisions that people increasingly face as they age. Nearly four-in-ten U.S. adults (37%) say they have given a great deal of thought to their wishes for medical treatment at the end of their lives, and an additional 35% have given some thought to these issues. But fully a quarter of adults (27%) say they have not given very much thought or have given no thought at all to how they would like doctors and other medical professionals to handle their medical treatment at the end of their lives.

Even among Americans ages 75 and older, one-in-four say they have not given very much or any thought to their end-of-life wishes. Further, one-in-five Americans ages 75 and older (22%) say they have neither written down nor talked with someone about their wishes for medical treatment at the end of their lives. And three-in-ten of those who describe their health as fair or poor have neither written down nor talked about their wishes with anyone, according to the Pew Research survey.

There has been only modest change over time in the level of public attention to, and preparation for, end-of-life medical decisions. The share of Americans who report having given a great deal of thought to their own wishes for end-of-life medical treatment (37%) is roughly the same as it was in a 2005 Pew Research Center survey and up modestly from 23 years ago, when 28% said they had given a great deal of thought to their wishes. About a third of all adults (35%) say they have put their wishes for end-of-life decisions into writing, whether in an informal document (such as a letter to a relative) or a formal, legal one (such as a living will or health care directive). That share is about the same as in 2005 (34%) and up from about one-in-six (16%) in 1990.

The vast majority of people *who have given a great deal of thought to their own wishes* have either written down or talked about their wishes with someone else (88%). Conversely, only about three-in-ten (31%) of those who say they have not given very much or any thought to their wishes have written down or talked about their wishes.

Americans with more education and higher incomes are more likely than those with less education and lower incomes to have communicated their wishes for end-of-life care. Whites are more likely than blacks or Hispanics to have made their wishes known. Those who have not written down or talked about their wishes are more likely than those who have made their wishes known to say they would want doctors and nurses to do everything possible to keep them alive if they were facing a dire medical situation.

Attention to, preparation for and preferences about end-of-life medical treatments also are correlated with age. Younger adults, especially those ages 18–49, are less likely than their older counterparts to have thought about these issues and to have put their wishes for end-of-life treatment in writing. Younger generations also are less inclined to say they would tell their doctors to stop treatment if they were facing a serious illness. Differences in personal preferences among Americans ages 50 and older are relatively muted, however. For example, if faced with an incurable disease and experiencing a great deal of pain, six-in-ten or more of those ages 50–64, 65–74, and 75 and older say they would tell their doctors to stop treatment so they could die, while 22–24% of each age group says they would tell their doctors to do everything possible to save their lives in those circumstances.

A Variety of Views

Other findings from the survey include:

- Many Americans have faced end-of-life medical issues through experiences with friends or relatives. About half of adults (47%) say they have a friend or relative who has had a terminal illness or who has been in a coma within the last five years. This experience cuts across most social and demographic groups, including age, gender, education and religious affiliation. And about half of these adults (23% of the general public) report that the issue of withholding life-sustaining treatment arose for their loved one.

- A strong majority of the public (78%) says that a close family member should be allowed to make decisions on behalf of a patient toward the end of life if the patient is unable to communicate his or her own wishes. At the same time, a substantial minority of adults (38%) say that parents have a right to refuse treatment on behalf of an infant born with a life-threatening defect, while 57% say such an infant should receive as much treatment as possible, regardless of the defect.

- In an aging society, Americans see a number of characteristics and functions as important to a good quality of life. About half of adults (49%) rate being able to talk or communicate as extremely important for a good quality of life in older age; similar shares say being able to feed oneself (45%), getting enjoyment out of life (44%) and living without severe, long-lasting pain (43%) are extremely important for a good quality of life in older age. Adults ages 75 and older are less inclined than younger generations to rate seven of the eight characteristics included in the survey as important for a good quality of life.

The Rights of Patients Support Physician Aid in Dying

John M. Grohol

John M. Grohol is a psychologist and the founder and chief executive officer of the website Psych Central. He is also an author, researcher, and expert in the intersection of technology and mental health.

Dr. Ron Pies writes an eloquent defense of why physician-assisted suicide should not be made a legal right in Massachusetts. He compares it to a doctor helping one of his patients jump from a bridge—something most doctors would never do.

Death with Dignity

But in making this analogy, I believe we're removing all context and logic from the decision behind wanting to end your own life because of a terminal illness. For the patient, it's not about the act of suicide or ending their lives—it's about alleviating suffering from the disease and choosing one's own way of dying with a little dignity. It's about patient empowerment, human dignity and choice.

That's why in the two states where it is legal for doctors to help patients with a terminal illness, it's referred to as the Death with Dignity law.

Because the alternative takes much of the dignity out of dying in today's modern medical system.

The Pain and Suffering of Death

"Physicians have no more business helping patients kill themselves with lethal drugs than they do helping patients jump off bridges," says Dr. Pies.

Most would agree physicians have little business helping a person jump to their death. But it appears that Dr. Pies undermines his own argument when he suggests it is perfectly okay for a physician to let his or her patient die of willful starvation and dehydration. His rationale? Death this way is solely in the patient's hands, and isn't as painful as we imagine it to be. He points to the scientific evidence, because there have been studies assessing patients' pain and suffering as they're dying through starvation and dehydration. Well, no, not quite. The evidence he points to is a single study that surveyed—not patients—but *hospice nurses.*

Now while I have great respect for the work and opinions of hospice nurses, let's not confuse their opinions with data that would be more helpful—*from the patients themselves.* But there is no such data. So we don't honestly know—and can't say—whether a patient whose doctor is okay with letting them starve themselves to death is in greater or lesser pain than one whose doctor has voluntarily prescribed a medication to hasten a terminal patient's death.

Just as most physicians do not perform abortions, I suspect many physicians will also not be interested in prescribing drugs to help a person at the end of their life hasten their own death.

Dr. Pies seems to be splitting hairs here. His objection appears to be that patients can end their lives if done solely on their own, because physicians shouldn't help patients along to their death—especially with a prescription. Yet he's okay with a patient starving themselves to death—something no physician would *ever* be okay with in any other situation (such as a patient who had anorexia).

Physicians of such starving patients don't just leave at that point. They too *actively help* the patient starve themselves by alleviating the discomfort associated with starving and dehydration. Physicians do this by prescribing a sedative, a practice known as *terminal sedation* or *palliative sedation*.

It's not that starving to death isn't a painful process (it is)—*it's because the patient has been prescribed drugs—by a physician—to make their "natural" death less painful.*

No Obligation for Physicians

Last, Dr. Pies argues it is not a *right* to die with dignity at the end of our lives, in the time and manner of our choosing. But nobody is coercing physicians to comply with the proposed law in Massachusetts. Just as most physicians do not perform abortions, I suspect many physicians will also not be interested in prescribing drugs to help a person at the end of their life hasten their own death.

We need such a law not to compel physicians or mess with their moral code, but because government has determined that the people cannot be trusted to have access to certain medications. Because government has restricted our access to such drugs, it is necessary to seek access to them through the government- and guild-defined methods imposed.

If my liberty to purchase and administer such drugs wasn't restricted in the first place, we wouldn't need such laws. *But since my liberty has been restricted, a law is needed.* This law would *not* impose an obligation on physicians to prescribe such medications to any patient who asked, as it would be completely voluntary for physicians to participate:

(2) Participation in this chapter shall be voluntary. If a health care provider is unable or unwilling to carry out a

patient's request under this chapter, and the patient transfers his or her care to a new health care provider, the prior health care provider shall transfer, upon request, a copy of the patient's relevant medical records to the new health care provider.

One of a physician's primary purposes is to help alleviate suffering. Suggesting a patient starve themselves over a period of one to two weeks, while being prescribed and administered a sedative, hardly seems in the spirit of this purpose.

For me, it's not about a physician's rights—it's about a human being's inalienable rights and having the right to choose. So I will be voting "Yes" on Question 2 for the Death with Dignity Act in Massachusetts [voters rejected the measure with 51% against it, in November 2012]. Because I believe that people with a terminal illness have a right to die at a time and place of their own choosing—with the dignity deserving of a human life.

Should Doctors Participate in Executions?

Ty Alper, interviewed by Rachel Martin

Ty Alper is a clinical professor of law at the University of California, Berkeley School of Law. Rachel Martin is the host of Weekend Edition Sunday on National Public Radio (NPR).

*R*achel Martin: The execution of a death row inmate in Oklahoma this past week [April 29, 2014] has reignited the debate over the use of lethal injection in this country. According to reporters at the scene, Clayton Lockett writhed in pain after receiving the lethal combination of drugs. He had a heart attack 43 minutes later, and died. On Friday, President Obama called the execution, quote, "deeply troubling," and ordered the Department of Justice to review how the death penalty is applied across the country.

The Oklahoma execution has also raised a lot of questions about what kind of medical oversight happens in state executions. Is a medical professional always there to monitor how the inmate responds to the drugs? To talk more about this, we spoke with Ty Alper, a clinical professor of law at the University of California, Berkeley, who has represented death row inmates. And we asked him if participating in an execution, as some have argued, is a violation of medical ethics.

Ty Alper: Well, most medical associations—the American Medical Association and state-based medical associations—have ethical guidelines that prohibit the participation of doctors in executions. But it's important to keep in mind that those are just the guidelines of those medical associations.

And the majority of doctors are not members of those associations. So the guidelines don't have any enforcement teeth.

Some in the medical community say that doctors who participate in state executions should actually lose their licenses. This past week, a man named Sidney Wolfe, a physician and consumer advocate, said, quote, "it's reprehensible when a physician deliberately participates in any way in the intentional killing of another human being by involvement in an execution." You, yourself, oppose the death penalty. Do you agree with him?

I don't agree with him. I think—I am opposed to the death penalty, and I don't think that we should be executing people. But if we are, and particularly if we're going to do it by way of procedures that are shrouded in secrecy, that use experimental combinations of drugs that have never been used before, then we need to have competent medical personnel involved.

And I think that courts should require that qualified, competent medical personnel participate. That doesn't mean that any particular doctor should be forced to participate in an execution. But if a person is going to be executed, there should be qualified people on hand.

I think it runs the gamut why doctors participate [in executions of death row inmates]. But they certainly do, in many cases.

So at this point, that is not a mandate for every state. It's up to each state to decide whether or not they have some kind of medical oversight?

That's correct. For the most part, courts have shied away from doing that, in part because states have successfully argued to courts that it's impossible to find doctors who are willing to do it. In fact, we know that doctors participate in all sorts of ways for a variety of reasons.

What are some of those reasons?

I've never spoken with a doctor who has participated in an execution, but there have been interviews. And for the most part, the doctors who were willing to discuss it say that they view it, in a way, as similar to terminal illness. And they can relieve suffering, and that they feel that it's their duty to relieve suffering. I don't know if that's the case for all doctors who participate, so I think it runs the gamut why doctors participate. But they certainly do, in many cases.

A doctor was on hand during the execution of Clayton Lockett in Oklahoma. But his role in the events remains unclear, at this point. Do you think this is a case—from what you know—where a physician could have helped the situation?

In the case of what happened in Oklahoma Tuesday night, we just don't know enough about what happened because everything about that execution was shrouded in secrecy. And it will take a truly independent review to determine what happened.

You talk a lot about the need to make sure that there are qualified medical professionals who are on hand during state executions. What are those qualifications? What does someone need to know in order to be effective in this role?

To be simplistic about it, they need to be good doctors. They need to know what they're doing. They need to have the training and experience to perform the . . .

You think they need to be doctors; they need to be MDs.

I don't think they necessarily need to be medical doctors. It depends on what they're doing. In the case of Clayton Lockett, we now know that the phlebotomist, who's not a medical doctor, was unable to find a peripheral IV line. And so the doctor had to come in and set what's called a femoral line, in the groin.

That's a much more difficult procedure, much more sensitive procedure. It's a painful procedure that has to be done, usually, by a qualified medical doctor. Again, we don't know exactly what went wrong in Oklahoma, but it appears that

that central line may not have been set properly. So if a doctor is going to be called to do that particular task, he or she needs to be qualified to do it, and trained well to do it.

It Is Time to Integrate Abortion into Primary Care

Susan Yanow

Susan Yanow is consultant to a number of reproductive rights and health organizations that work to advance access to abortion, including the Reproductive Health Access Project (RHAP).

The *Roe v Wade* decision made safe abortion available but did not change the reality that more than 1 million women face an unwanted pregnancy every year. Forty years after *Roe v Wade*, the procedure is not accessible to many US women.

The Politics of Abortion

The politics of abortion have led to a plethora of laws that create enormous barriers to abortion access, particularly for young, rural, and low-income women. Family medicine physicians and advanced practice clinicians are qualified to provide abortion care.

To realize the promise of *Roe v Wade*, first-trimester abortion must be integrated into primary care and public health professionals and advocates must work to remove barriers to the provision of abortion within primary care settings.

The 1973 *Roe v Wade* decision removed many legal obstacles to abortion and was a public health watershed. The availability of safe abortion services led to dramatically decreased rates of maternal morbidity and mortality in the United States, as in most countries that have removed legal impediments to abortion care.

Susan Yanow, "It Is Time to Integrate Abortion Into Primary Care," *American Journal of Public Health*, vol. 103, no. 1, 2013, pp. 14–16. Copyright © 2013 American Public Health Association. All rights reserved. Reproduced with permission.

According to the most recent available data, approximately 1.2 million women obtain safe, legal abortions from skilled clinicians in the United States every year. The political debate over abortion has largely ignored the public health fact that the *Roe v Wade* decision did not create or change the need for abortion; legalization simply made abortion safe. Maternal death from unsafe abortion in the United States became a negligible statistic after 1973. Abortion is now one of the safest medical procedures available; only 0.3% of abortion patients experience a complication that requires hospitalization.

The skills needed to provide abortions ... are in the scope of practice of primary clinicians.

Unwanted pregnancy continues to be a reality of women's lives. One in three women in the United States will seek an abortion before she is aged 45 years. For these women, restrictive laws driven by ideology, not science, are undermining the promise of *Roe v Wade* in many parts of the country. State restrictions—including waiting periods, parental consent requirements for minors, lack of insurance coverage or Medicaid coverage for abortion, and expensive and unnecessary building requirements for facilities that provide abortions—create almost insurmountable barriers to access, especially for rural, young, and low-income women. There are ever-increasing restrictions passed at the state and federal levels, and antiabortion activists have directed a relentless campaign of violence and harassment at clinics and clinicians who provide the service. Many medical residencies lack training opportunities, leading to a lack of skilled abortion providers. The cumulative result of these regulations, the harassment, and the lack of training is a shrinking number of sites that offer abortion services.

Specialized abortion clinics performed 70% of all abortions in 2008, yet the hostile political climate those opposed to abortion have created is forcing the numbers of these clinics to decline every year. The number of abortion providers has declined dramatically, from 2908 in 1982 to 1787 in 2005. Eighty-seven percent of all US counties lacked an abortion provider in 2008; 35% of US women live in those counties. Abortion services are concentrated in cities. Almost all non-metropolitan counties (which is 97% of all US counties) lack an abortion provider. In eight states (Arkansas, Idaho, Mississippi, Missouri, North Dakota, Oklahoma, South Dakota, and Wyoming) there are abortion clinics in only one city in the entire state. The result of the shortage of providers is that although abortion is one of the most common medical procedures performed in the United States, in many areas of the country women must travel for hours and deal with long delays to get the reproductive health care they need.

Studies have shown that abortion care that family doctors provide have low rates of complication and that many patients would prefer to get their abortion from their family physician.

The Practice of Primary Care Clinicians

Primary care clinicians provide personalized continuous preventative health care to patients throughout their reproductive years. Physician assistants, nurse midwives, and nurse practitioners (collectively, advanced practice clinicians, or APCs) and family physicians provide the majority of well-woman care to patients throughout the country. The skills needed to provide abortions—including the ability to assess gestational age, provide counseling, provide medications, perform manual or electric vacuum aspiration, and conduct post-abortion follow-up—are in the scope of practice of primary clinicians. Many primary care clinicians who specialize in women's health have specialized training. They perform suturing, colposcopy, intrauterine device insertions, endometrial biopsy, and gynecological care; and prescribe medications for family planning. These skills are comparable to those required to perform a first-trimester abortion.

The provision of first-trimester abortion care is clearly within the scope of practice of primary care clinicians. In fact, since 1973 physician assistants have provided abortions in Montana and Vermont. Beginning in the early 1990s, advocates and professional groups came together to begin state-by-state advocacy to clarify the laws and scope of practice issues and promote the involvement of APCs in abortion care. APCs have been legally recognized as competent to substitute for physicians in the performance of many tasks. Several studies have compared complication rates and patient satisfaction between abortions physicians provide and those APCs provide. These studies consistently show that APCs with the requisite skills, training, and experience are fully competent to provide medical and first-trimester surgical abortions safely. As a result of state-by-state advocacy, APCs are now providing medication abortion in 18 states. APCs provide aspiration abortions in Montana, New Hampshire, Oregon, and Vermont.

Additionally, APCs are providing aspiration abortion in California through a five-year demonstration project (Health Workforce Pilot Project No. 171) under the auspices of the University of California, San Francisco. Nurse practitioners, certified nurse midwives, and physician assistants have been trained to provide first-trimester aspiration abortion, and the project is being carefully evaluated. To date, 41 APCs at sites across California have been trained through the project. Nearly 8000 patients have received abortion care from these trained nurse practitioners, certified nurse midwives, and physician assistants. The project has conducted a study to compare the outcomes of these early abortions that APCs performed to a comparable number that physicians performed. The data show similar rates of high patient satisfaction and low complications in both groups.

Nurse practitioners, certified nurse midwives, and physician assistants have been increasing their commitment to abortion care, and there has also been remarkable advocacy among family medicine physicians. Several organizations (e.g., the Reproductive Health Access Project and the Center for Reproductive Health Education in Family Medicine [RHEDI]) have worked to increase training in abortion procedures in family medicine residency programs and to increase advocacy among family medicine professional organizations. Family physicians currently provide abortions at many of the freestanding clinics around the United States. Studies have shown that abortion care that family doctors provide have low rates of complication and that many patients would prefer to get their abortion from their family physician.

Integration of Abortion into Primary Care

As more primary care clinicians are being trained and expressing interest in providing abortions, new technologies are making it possible for women to diagnose and end their pregnancies earlier. Inexpensive and accurate pregnancy tests now allow many women to determine whether they are pregnant within two weeks after unprotected intercourse. Advances in ultrasound have made it possible to confirm a pregnancy very early on. These advances have contributed to women in the first trimester coming in earlier to end an unwanted pregnancy. Eighty-eight percent of women who have abortions get the procedure in the first 12 weeks of pregnancy, and 61.8% of women have their abortion before the ninth week. All these women could be treated in a primary care setting.

Yet most of the primary care clinicians who currently provide abortions do so at freestanding abortion sites. Too often when a patient seeks an abortion from her primary care clinician at her medical home, she is referred to another health care provider, even though trained family medicine doctors, nurse practitioners, certified nurse midwives, and physician assistants can provide first-trimester abortions. Although there are certainly primary care clinicians who do not want to provide abortions to their patients, many qualified and trained clinicians are willing but unable to offer this care because of burdensome, politically motivated restrictions that are not derived from science, public health considerations, or good medicine.

> *Family doctors who want to provide early abortion care in their practices must purchase extremely expensive obstetrical coverage.*

Family medicine practices and physicians and community health centers are key health access points for low-income and rural women. Community health centers are the medical and health care home for more than 20 million people nationally, and community health center patients are disproportionately low income, uninsured or publicly insured, and minority. If abortion care were available in these centers and in family medicine practices, more women would be able to end their unwanted pregnancies without having to travel hundreds of miles or face delays that push them into getting abortions later in their pregnancy.

Unfortunately, most federally qualified community health centers do not offer abortion services because of the Hyde Amendment, a legislative provision barring the use of federal funds to pay for abortions. Additionally, many of the federally qualified community health centers rely on malpractice coverage from the federal government, which does not cover abortion care. Family doctors who want to provide early abortion care in their practices must purchase extremely expensive obstetrical coverage, even though many other procedures routinely performed in family medicine have a higher complication rate than do first-trimester abortion procedures. APCs face other barriers; in many states, APCs are prevented from providing abortions or are limited to providing only medication abortion because of laws promoted by those who seek to restrict abortion access and because of resistance to expanding the scope of APCs' practice to include abortion care. The World Health Organization recently issued technical and policy guidelines for safe abortion worldwide. The guidelines state,

> Both vacuum aspiration and medical abortion can be provided at the primary care level on an outpatient basis and do not require advanced technical knowledge or skills, expensive equipment such as ultrasound, or a full complement of hospital staff (e.g., anaesthesiologist).

The United States needs to step up to the World Health Organization standard. Health care reform has identified the importance of promoting high-quality, continuous, accessible, and cost-effective care in primary care settings. It is time for the promise of legal abortion to be available to every woman in the United States, rural or urban, low-income or middle class. Public health professionals and advocates must work together to find strategies to expand access to abortion by removing restrictions on the primary care clinicians who are trained and willing to provide the service. Forty years after *Roe v Wade*, it is time to integrate first-trimester abortion into primary care.

Medical Professionals Should Not Have to Participate in the Taking of Life

Wesley J. Smith

Wesley J. Smith is a senior fellow at the Discovery Institute's Center on Human Exceptionalism and consults for the Patients Rights Council and the Center for Bioethics and Culture.

Fifty years ago, doctors would have been excoriated professionally for assisting a patient's suicide or performing a non-therapeutic abortion. After all, the Hippocratic Oath proscribed both practices, while the laws of most states made them felonies.

My, how times have changed. Today, abortion is a national constitutional right, and two states have passed laws legalizing doctor-prescribed death. Meanwhile, destroying human embryos may become the basis for cellular medical treatments and people diagnosed with a persistent vegetative state could, one day, be killed for their organs—a proposal often made to alleviate the organ shortage in some of the world's most notable bioethics and medical journals.

The Rights of Medical Professionals

With life-*taking* procedures threatening to become as much a part of medicine as life-saving techniques, a cogent question arises: What about the rights of doctors, nurses and other medical professionals who believe in traditional Hippocratic ethics? Increasingly those who do are castigated as interfering with "patient rights." Indeed, medical professionals may one day be forced to choose between their careers and their morals.

Actually, that day has already arrived in some parts of the world. For example, the state of Victoria, Australia, requires all doctors to either perform abortions or be complicit in the pregnancy termination by forcing morally objecting doctors to refer their abortion-seeking patients to doctors they know will do the deed. That requirement has already impacted the lives of some pro-life physicians. When I toured Australia speaking against legalizing euthanasia in July 2010, I met several who moved away from their homes in Victoria solely to avoid being forced to choose between their morality and their professions.

Under the terms of the Stormans *case, all pharmacies [in Washington State] would be required to knowingly dispense death-causing drugs for use in legal assisted suicide.*

Victoria's formula may soon be copied in other countries. Euthanasia is legal in the Netherlands, for example, but doctors are not yet required by law to kill. But that protection is eroding. Recently, the Dutch Medical Association (KNMG) released an ethics directive about euthanasia that, like Victoria's abortion law, requires objecting doctors to refer legally qualified euthanasia-requesting patients to doctors willing to administer the lethal jab. This is the same KNMG, by the way, that pointedly also allows doctors to provide how-to-commit-suicide information to suicidal patients not qualified for legal euthanasia.

The Anti-Conscience Movement

Surely, such coercion would never happen in the USA. Alas, the anti-conscience tide is already flowing. A few years ago, Washington State promulgated a regulation requiring pharmacies to dispense all legal prescriptions. The Catholic owners of a small pharmaceutical chain sued, claiming that the rule forced them to provide the morning after pill in contravention of their religious beliefs. The Ninth Circuit Court of Appeals was entirely unsympathetic, ruling in *Stormans v. Selecky* that the law was generally applicable, and hence, the owners' freedom of religion had not been violated.

That decision is relevant to whether medical professionals can be forced to participate in the taking of human life. Here's how: Washington legalized physician-assisted suicide in 2008. Thus, under the terms of the *Stormans* case, all pharmacies would be required to knowingly dispense death-causing drugs for use in legal assisted suicide. (Washington regulators are rewriting the regulation, which is, for now, suspended. But the appellate court's reasoning remains the law throughout the Ninth Circuit.)

It is becoming increasingly clear that medical professionals ... will face increasing pressure to yield their consciences to the desires of patients and the reigning moral cultural paradigm.

The increasing hostility to medical conscience rights was demonstrated vividly by the furor unleashed after the [George W.] Bush administration promulgated a rule explicitly protecting health care workers from workplace discrimination if they refuse to participate in a medical procedure that violates their conscience. Several medical associations objected. So did some medical journals. For example, an editorial in the April 9, 2009 *New England Journal of Medicine* urged revoking the Bush rule, stating, "health care providers—and all those whose jobs affect patient care—should cast off the cloak of conscience when patients' needs demand it."

Unsurprisingly, the mainstream media jumped with both feet into the anti-conscience bandwagon. *The New York Times* called the protections "an awful regulation," while *The St. Louis Post Dispatch* went so far as to state, "Doctors, nurses, pharmacists choose professions that put patients' rights first. If they foresee that priority becoming problematic for them, they should choose another profession."

In other words, the *Dispatch* editorialists believe that health care professionals should be forced to choose between killing in abortion, assisted suicide or other potentially lethal procedures, and their careers.

The Need to Protect Medical Conscience

In the face of such implacable opposition, the Bush protections didn't last long. One of the new [Barack] Obama administration first official acts began the process of revoking the Bush rule, which fell last February [2011]—although some aspects of federal law still protect against forced participation in abortion.

It is becoming increasingly clear that medical professionals who wish to continue in the Hippocratic tradition will face increasing pressure to yield their consciences to the desires of patients and the reigning moral cultural paradigm. The question thus becomes what to do about it.

Ironically, some in Europe have already begun the task of protecting medical professionals who don't want to kill. The Council of Europe recently passed "The Right to Conscientious Objection in Lawful Medical Care," which states in part:

> No person, hospital or institution shall be coerced, held liable or discriminated against in any manner because of a refusal to perform, accommodate, assist or submit to an abortion, the performance of a human miscarriage, or euthanasia or any act which could cause the death of a human foetus or embryo, for any reason.

This is the exactly right approach. We live in an increasingly morally polyglot society about matters of life, death and the overarching purposes of medicine. Death-causing procedures—or treatments derived from the destruction of human life—may well become more widely and legally available in the coming years. But just because something is legal, that doesn't mean it is right. The time has come for Congress and state legislatures to follow the lead of the Council of Europe and pass strong laws protecting medical conscience. Doctors, nurses, pharmacists and other medical professionals should not be forced to comport their professional conduct with the lowest common ethical denominator.

It Is an Ethics Violation for Doctors to Perform Death Penalty Executions

Ford Vox

Ford Vox is a physician and journalist.

Despite international human rights appeals and a conflicting Supreme Court ruling, on Monday Georgia intends to execute a mentally disabled man convicted of two murders [scheduled for July 15, 2013, but postponed due to a legal challenge]. When the lethal drug is pushed, the Medical Association of Georgia will be standing behind the doctor who will be making one of Georgia's most questionable executions possible. The medical association failed to enact its own membership ethics code for seven years and accredited the prison where the death will occur, leaving the organization morally linked to this grave moment.

Doctor Participation in the Death Penalty

Though the European Union has intentionally created lethal injection drug shortages as part of its strategy to cripple America's capacity for capital punishment, the Peach State has persevered past this pharmaceutical blockade and will instead employ a single agent, pentobarbital. Pentoparbital's lone use means a longer and more uncertain death for the condemned man, Warren Hill, who will drift into an ever-deepening coma under the auspices of Dr. Carlo Musso and his team of doctors and nurses from Rainbow Medical Associates. Rainbow Medical shares the same address and the same key personnel as CorrectHealth, Dr. Musso's contract correctional health care company which provides medical services to jails and prisons throughout Georgia. CorrectHealth personnel both mend prisoners and finish them off.

Doctors who participate in executions in Georgia and other states have survived repeated challenges to their medical licenses lodged by anti-death penalty activists. Capital punishment is legal, and death penalty states provide added immunity (and anonymity if desired) to cooperating medical personnel. Last summer the Southern Center for Human Rights [SCHR] decided to try another approach and challenge Dr. Musso's importation of sodium thiopental via Drug Enforcement Agency [DEA]-unregulated back channels. Though the DEA seized Georgia's sodium thiopental supply, it appears nothing will come of SCHR's complaint to the medical board, likely due to the special immunity doctors participating in capital punishment receive.

AMA members must remain dedicated to our ethical obligations that prohibit involvement in capital punishment.

While his medical license is safe, Dr. Musso is not a welcome character in the American Medical Association [AMA] due to his violations of its Principles of Medical Ethics which specifically proscribe activities even indirectly associated with enacting capital punishment. Unethical conduct includes examining the condemned for mental fitness, selecting drugs and doses, starting IVs, reading EKGs, and pronouncing death. Dr. Musso and his team handle all technical aspects surrounding the procedure except for physically pushing the drug(s). There is no moral distinction in that omission, according to the AMA.

This attitude certainly fits with the experience of most doctors who are accustomed to seeing others physically carry out their orders. Though a number of press reports cite his

AMA membership—and even a 2010 Georgia state senate resolution commending his career in correctional health states he's a member—the AMA says otherwise. If he were on their membership rolls, the AMA would call a hearing that could lead to his suspension or expulsion.

Though AMA policy doesn't allow it to divulge the details of such proceedings, Dr. Musso himself disclosed that his AMA membership was under assault in a 2006 interview. "The use of a physician's clinical skill and judgment for purposes other than promoting an individual's health and welfare undermines a central ethical pillar of medicine—first, do no harm," said AMA president Dr. Jeremy Lazarus. "AMA members must remain dedicated to our ethical obligations that prohibit involvement in capital punishment."

After the last medical executionist signed off in 2004 in a wave of bad publicity and license challenges filed by anti-death penalty activists, Georgia was in need of someone new. State corrections officials asked physicians at Georgia Health Sciences University to assist with the lethal injection procedure, said university spokeswoman Jennifer Scott. The university already provides most prison health care. Physicians there, charged with training medical students and residents, pointed out that participation would violate their core professional ethics and jeopardize their standing in the profession. They respectfully declined.

A Doctor's Personal Morality

Dr. Musso has scaffolded his own unique rationalizations around the issue. Personally, he is opposed to the death penalty. Capital punishment is just another terminal condition, he rationalizes. He joins in because he just wants to see it done right. That may very well be the case. Of note, though, doing it right does mean that his four staff members divide up an $18,000 payment for each procedure.

If Dr. Musso is indeed personally uncomfortable with capital punishment, he is probably especially tentative about contentious cases like that of the mentally disabled man scheduled to die on Monday night. But he and his team have followed through on their state contract since 2004 on quite a number of contested cases, including Troy Davis.

Dr. Musso may be willing to whittle down his own internal morality, but organized medicine doesn't have to submit to his logic. On a national level, medicine's covered. He's unwelcome in the AMA. But what about the Georgia state affiliate of the AMA, the Medical Association of Georgia (MAG)?

Dr. Musso's company bio touts his MAG membership, and MAG confirmed his active membership. Yet MAG adopted the AMA's ethics policy on capital punishment in 2005. Dr. Musso has been on the record assisting executions since that year as well, as first reported in the *Atlanta Journal Constitution*. Why has MAG stood behind Dr. Musso all these years? "MAG is not aware of any MAG members or Georgia Department of Corrections staff that are performing executions," MAG spokesperson Tom Kornegay said via email. I asked MAG to take *The Atlantic*'s inquiries as official notice that Dr. Musso is involved in aspects of execution specifically disallowed in MAG's own policy.

[The Medical Association of Georgia's] accreditation program appears to allow GDCP a way to provide accredited health care as required by the courts while maintaining its medicalized lethal injection regime.

In a tense conversation with MAG CEO Donald Palmisano Tuesday evening I requested that the organization distance itself from publicly known executionists like Dr. Musso. Mr. Palmisano stood his ground. I've heard nothing more from the organization.

MAG's Ethic Policy

The Medical Association of Georgia is intertwined with Monday's execution in another way the organization has been unwilling to address this week: it accredits the prison health care at the Georgia Diagnostic and Classification Prison (GDCP) where Warren Hill will die in a medical procedure. The standard bearer of correctional health systems evaluation is the National Commission on Correctional Health Care [NCCHC]. The NCCHC is the "Joint Commission" of the correctional health world, but they don't accredit a single Georgia prison, the NCCHC told me. Instead, MAG offers accreditation that's "consistent" with standards of the NCCHC, MAG's spokesperson told me. MAG was unwilling to state whether they accredit the GDCP, but Georgia Health Sciences University confirmed this information.

Perhaps MAG is unwilling to say more because the organization doesn't want to be unfairly linked to what medical staff do in that prison. But the link appears fair to me: the NCCHC itself is unwilling to accredit GDCP. I spoke to NCCHC Accreditation Compliance Specialist Mackenzie Bisset about it on Tuesday. Medical staff may not participate in executions, and "if a facility has medical personnel participating in executions they could not be accredited," Bisset said.

The Georgia Department of Corrections wouldn't talk this week, but a 2007 nursing magazine depicts Dr. Musso and one of his nurse employees providing care at the prison. MAG's NCCHC accreditation program appears to allow GDCP a way to provide accredited health care as required by the courts while maintaining its medicalized lethal injection regime.

As it stands, a member of the Medical Association of Georgia will provide his medical services as an execution specialist on Monday, just as he has publically acknowledged doing for the past seven years. This time his iatrogenically terminal patient is a mentally disabled man. MAG's seven-year-old ethics policy against doctors performing execution hasn't been enforced so far. MAG has an opportunity to declare that if Dr. Musso assists in Monday's execution, he'll be called in for a hearing and his membership may be revoked. By doing so, MAG will be issuing a statement to the world that Georgia's physicians will stand together to defend their profession's core ethical standards. Seven years of silence is enough.

Moral Disapproval of Abortion Justifies Doctor Refusal to Provide It

E. Christian Brugger

E. Christian Brugger is the J. Francis Cardinal Stafford Professor of Moral Theology at St. John Vianney Theological Seminary and senior fellow of ethics at the Culture of Life Foundation.

In November 2007 the American College of Obstetricians and Gynecologists (ACOG) published an opinion that if a woman's physical or mental health were at risk, medical practitioners had "an obligation" to provide "medically indicated" abortions "regardless of the provider's personal moral objections." It acknowledged that respect for consciences is important, but that "conscientious refusals should be limited if they constitute an imposition of religious or moral beliefs on patients."

The Right to Refuse Medical Care

The ACOG's opinion motivated the [George W.] Bush administration in summer 2008 to establish federal regulations meant to ensure that laws on the books protecting the right of health-care workers to conscientiously object to involvement in abortions and sterilizations would be duly enforced. The lame duck administration issued the regulations in December 2008. In March 2009, the new [Barack] Obama administration began a process of rescission. It argued the regulations were unnecessary because conscience laws were already adequately upheld in U.S. healthcare and that any positive goals they might achieve were likely to be accompanied by unacceptable harms such as restricting access to legal abortion for low-income women. The Obama administration formally rescinded the regulations in February 2011.

Given the numerous counterexamples, there are good reasons for rejecting the administration's argument that conscience laws are adequately enforced. But I do not pursue them here. Behind the controversy over the Bush regulations lies the more basic question of whether healthcare providers have a right to refuse to cooperate in medical procedures they judge to be wrong. And beneath this lies the question of the nature of conscience more generally. As far as I can see, the ACOG's conclusion has only one merit: it follows consistently from its prior account of conscience, an account that reduces the faculty to subjective feeling.

In this essay, I will elaborate the ACOG account, juxtapose it to what I call the "classical account" as defended in Western philosophy, and finally answer the question whether healthcare providers have a right to refuse to treat some patients. In addition to setting forth what I think is an account that is philosophically consistent and flexible enough to be useful in discussions of public policy, I hope also to shed light on the way the current administration understands conscience and the rights that attach to it. For it is unquestionably the case that Obama's account mirrors the ACOG's.

What happens when a conflict arises between my personal beliefs and the objective duty of my profession to provide patient-centered care?

The ACOG Opinion on Conscience

The ACOG refers to conscience as "the private, constant, ethically attuned part of the human character"; conscience acts as an "internal sanction" on action and inaction; it expresses itself in the form of "a sentiment" such as: "If I were to do 'x,' I could not live with myself/I would hate myself/I wouldn't be able to sleep at night"; not to direct action in accord with it is to "betray oneself—to risk personal wholeness or identity"; conscience is "authentic" when one believes that acting against it will cause one to "experience guilt, shame, or loss of self-respect."

According to this definition, the moral disapproval that conscience registers is essentially a strong feeling—a "sentiment"—of repugnance or self-reproach that I feel when I compare my beliefs about my own moral uprightness with contemplated behavior that I feel threatens those beliefs. Conscience protects this subjective sense, elliptically referred to as "moral integrity"; indeed, it is my "right" to protect it, for herein lies the "soundness, reliability, wholeness and integration of [one's] moral character."

What happens when a conflict arises between my personal beliefs and the objective duty of my profession to provide patient-centered care? Say, for example, that I am a pro-life ObGyn faced with an urgent request from a patient to abort her fetus. If conscientious refusal would constitute an imposition of my values on a patient who does not share them, and if refusal would negatively impact the well-being of the patient "as the patient perceives it," then the claims arising from my subjective sense should not be allowed to override my duty to the patient: "providers have an obligation to provide medically indicated and requested [abortions] regardless of the provider's personal moral objections."

Following this logic, our subjective moral sense and the faculty of conscience that enforces it apparently have nothing to do with objective right and wrong. But let's be clear: the ACOG's moral universe is not devoid of normativity. The opinion refers to performing abortions as an "obligation"; reproductive services "*should* be maintained"; conscience rights "*should not* be a pretext for interfering with patients' rights to [abortion] services"; and so on (emphases added). The opinion is full of normative assertions giving primacy to some judgments over others. But if judgments of conscience stretch no wider than sentiment, how is it that the ACOG justifies its own normative conclusions as superior to those of abortion opponents? On this, the opinion is mute.

However closely interconnected conscience is to human emotions, its judgments pitch themselves higher than affective states. They are judgments upon reality.

The Classical Conception of Conscience

In its classical understanding, conscience is an operation of reason—practical reason, interested in true knowledge for the sake of acting. Reasoning practically entails, first, a process of deliberation over interesting alternatives for action, and second, the judgment that this or that alternative is right or wrong, and consequently rightly or wrongly chosen. This presupposes a general cognitive framework of right and wrong. This framework—our moral knowledge—is not merely an affectively supported matrix of subjective beliefs, but the basic apprehension of a set of propositions asserting truths pertaining to what is good, choiceworthy, and consistent with human well-being. Practical reasoning, then, is the process of moving from these "general principles" to practical conclusions. The conclusions are judgments *hic et nunc* (here and now) that some rational proposal for acting is consistent or inconsistent with human good, and so is right or wrong. These judgments are acts of *conscience*.

So I exercise conscience whenever I consider what I or one for whom I have some responsibility, including a group, including the entire community the common good of which my good in part constitutes, should or should not do. Conscience entails the entire realm of practical deliberation and judgment.

Now insofar as its acts are the acts of a person (i.e., a primary source of moral agency), conscience's subjectivity is plain. But the propositional contents of its acts do not merely signify the experience of an emotional state: "I feel this is wrong." However closely interconnected conscience is to human emotions, its judgments pitch themselves higher than affective states. They are judgments upon reality: "X is right (wrong) and so should (should not) be done whether or not I feel like it." The realm of conscience, then, is the realm of the rationally normative. And is it not the case that squarely in the center of that realm sits the ACOG's judgment that providers sometimes have an obligation to provide abortions regardless of their personal moral objections? Do not its authors put it forward as normative—as true?

To the extent that they embody moral judgments about right action, conscience claims bind, even claims arising from self-deception, invidious opinions, and aesthetic repugnance.

What, then, is a "conscience objection"? An objection follows from a prior judgment that some option is wrong and should not be done. The objection is precisely my rational opposition to adopting that option. It is my unwillingness to do what I judge to be wrong. I may, of course, judge something wrong that is in fact quite innocent. It would not be innocent, however, for me to do it if I judged it in advance to be wrong. The epistemological basis of obligation is the judgment itself. In this account, wrongdoing is *chosen*—i.e., I am culpable for *doing* wrong—whenever I judge something to be wrong and then reject that judgment and do it; I do what I believe I should not do.

For this reason, conscience is said to be supreme in matters of action. If self-direction and hence responsibility exist and are not fictions, then judgments about good and evil must be the basis of right action. And they must be binding.

The Importance of Conscience

We can affirm, then, both that conscience errs and that its judgments always bind. They bind unless and until I come [upon], perhaps through further deliberation, new knowledge, or being disabused of some error, to a contrary judgment. Although positive judgments do not always command action, but rather sanction it ("X is legitimate and may rightly be done"), negative judgments always command here and now in the form of a prohibition ("Y should not be done").

To say that the duty to act consistently with my conscience is absolute is simply to say that I should only do what I judge to be legitimate and never do what I judge to be wrong. If this is the case, a negative conscience judgment on some type of behavior seals the imperative not to choose that behavior. Hence the proposition repeated in the ACOG opinion that some conscience claims are "not genuine" and should be disregarded seems to me false. To the extent that they embody moral judgments about right action, conscience claims bind, even claims arising from self-deception, invidious opinions, and aesthetic repugnance. This is no more than to say that the conscience judgments of morally immature people are binding. We overcome an immature conscience through education, not by denying that its claims are "genuine." It follows that healthcare workers never have a prior duty to carry out requests that they judge to be wrong.

Does it follow that every kind of conscience objection must be accommodated without any consequences to workers? Rightful accommodation certainly prohibits all forcible opposition. But it need not be incompatible with the expectation that reasonable duties will be carried out. Who decides what's reasonable? Ordinarily the question poses no conflict. When it does, for example, in the vexed arena of so-called "reproductive services," where orthodoxies clash, public policy needs to step in and give practical definition to the scope of reasonable conscience objection.

The Need to Protect Liberty of Conscience

For practical purposes, "conscience laws" are instituted to protect claims arising from negative conscience judgments. I suggest that if some kind of legally protected behavior elicits strong ethical disapproval from a significant percentage of responsible healthcare professionals, then conscientious objection from participation in that behavior should be protected under law. This includes, for example, activities associated with terminating fetal human life (e.g., undergoing, performing, assisting in the performance of, requiring or providing training in the performance of, providing referrals for, paying for, and providing coverage for abortions). It also includes the provision of contraceptive services, which elicits strong ethical disapproval from the largest non-governmental provider of health care in the United States, the Catholic Church.

The ACOG opinion suffers from gross illogic and ideological bias. It proposes that some moral judgments, namely, positive judgments related to procuring an abortion in emergency situations, not only sanction the choice for the abortion seeker, but apodictically command medical professionals to carry out that choice on the seeker's behalf, irrespective of their conscientious objections.

I have argued that moral obligation stems from the judgment of conscience; that negative judgments issue in exceptionless prohibitions; and that no professional obligation may override conscience's settled voice. Actions that elicit strong ethical disapproval from large numbers of people should be singled out by law as the protected subject matter of conscientious objection. Whatever one's own ethical judgment on those actions, political stability is better served erring on the side of liberty of conscience.

Organizations to Contact

The editors have compiled the following list of organizations concerned with the issues debated in this book. The descriptions are derived from materials provided by the organizations. All have publications or information available for interested readers. The list was compiled on the date of publication of the present volume; names, addresses, phone and fax numbers, and e-mail and Internet addresses may change. Be aware that many organizations take several weeks or longer to respond to inquiries, so allow as much time as possible.

American Society of Law, Medicine, and Ethics (ASLME)
765 Commonwealth Ave., Suite 1634, Boston, MA 02215
(617) 262-4990 • fax: (617) 437-7596
e-mail: info@aslme.org
website: www.aslme.org

The American Society of Law, Medicine, and Ethics (ASLME) is a nonprofit educational organization focused on the intersection of law, medicine, and ethics. ASLME aims to provide a forum to exchange ideas in order to protect public health, reduce health disparities, promote quality of care, and facilitate dialogue on emerging science. ASMLE publishes two journals: *Journal of Law, Medicine & Ethics* and *American Journal of Law & Medicine*.

The Center for Bioethics & Human Dignity (CBHD)
Trinity International University
2065 Half Day Rd., Deerfield, IL 60015
(847) 317-8180 • fax: (847) 317-8101
e-mail: info@cbhd.org
website: www.cbhd.org

The Center for Bioethics & Human Dignity (CBHD) is a Christian bioethics research center at Trinity International University that explores the nexus of biomedicine, biotechnology, and humanity. CBHD works to equip thought leaders to engage the issues of bioethics using the tools of rigorous research, conceptual analysis, charitable critique, leading-edge publication, and effective teaching. CBHD publishes the quarterly journal *Dignitas*.

Center for Genetics and Society (CGS)

1936 University Ave., Suite 350, Berkeley, CA   94704
(510) 665-7760 • fax: (510) 665-8760
e-mail: info@geneticsandsociety.org
website: www.geneticsandsociety.org

The Center for Genetics and Society (CGS) is a nonprofit information and public affairs organization working to encourage responsible uses and effective societal governance of the new human genetic and reproductive technologies. CGS works with scientists, health professionals, and civil society leaders to oppose applications of new human genetic and reproductive technologies. CGS publishes reports, articles, and the newsletter *Biopolitical Views & News*, many of which are available at its website.

Council for Responsible Genetics (CRG)

5 Upland Rd., Suite 3, Cambridge, MA   02140
(617) 868-0870 • fax: (617) 491-5344
e-mail: crg@gene-watch.org
website: www.councilforresponsiblegenetics.org

The Council for Responsible Genetics (CRG) is a nonprofit organization dedicated to fostering public debate about the social, ethical, and environmental implications of genetic technologies. CRG works through the media and concerned citizens to distribute accurate information and represent the public interest on emerging issues in biotechnology. CRG publishes *GeneWatch*, a magazine dedicated to monitoring biotechnology's social, ethical, and environmental consequences.

Ethics and Public Policy Center (EPPC)

1730 M St. NW, Suite 910, Washington, DC   20036
(202) 682-1200 • fax: (202) 408-0632
e-mail: ethics@eppc.org
website: www.eppc.org

The Ethics and Public Policy Center (EPPC) is dedicated to applying the Judeo-Christian moral tradition to critical issues of public policy. Through its core programs, such as Bioethics and American Democracy, EPPC and its scholars work to influence policy makers and to transform the culture through the world of ideas. EPPC publishes *The New Atlantis*, a quarterly journal about technology with an emphasis on bioethics.

The Hastings Center

21 Malcolm Gordon Rd., Garrison, NY   10524-4125
(845) 424-4040 • fax: (845) 424-4545
e-mail: mail@thehastingscenter.org
website: www.thehastingscenter.org

The Hastings Center is a nonprofit bioethics research institute that works to address fundamental ethical issues in the areas of health, medicine, and the environment as they affect individuals, communities, and societies. The Hastings Center conducts research and education and collaborates with policy makers to identify and analyze the ethical dimensions of their work. The Center publishes two periodicals: *Hastings Center Report* and *IRB: Ethics & Human Research*.

Kennedy Institute of Ethics

Joseph and Rose Kennedy Institute of Ethics
Healy, 4th Floor, Georgetown University
Washington, DC   20057
(202) 687-0360
website: https://kennedyinstitute.georgetown.edu

The Kennedy Institute of Ethics at Georgetown University is the world's oldest academic bioethics center. The Kennedy Institute is home to a group of scholars who engage in research, teaching, and public service on issues such as health-care reform, death and dying, clinical research ethics, and abortion. It publishes the *Kennedy Institute of Ethics Journal*, which offers a scholarly forum for diverse views on major issues in bioethics.

Physicians for a National Health Program (PNHP)

29 E. Madison, Suite 602, Chicago, IL   60602
(312) 782-6006 • fax: (312) 782-6007
e-mail: info@pnhp.org
website: www.pnhp.org

Physicians for a National Health Program (PNHP) is a single-issue organization advocating a universal, comprehensive single-payer national health system in the United States. PNHP performs research on the need for fundamental health-care system reform, coordinates speakers and forums, participates in town hall meetings and debates, contributes scholarly articles to peer-reviewed medical journals, and appears regularly on national television and news programs advocating for a single-payer system. PNHP has a variety of articles available at its website, including many editorials written by its members.

Bibliography

Books

Roberto Abadie — *The Professional Guinea Pig: Big Pharma and the Risky World of Human Subjects.* Durham, NC: Duke University Press, 2010.

Alastair V. Campbell — *Bioethics: The Basics.* New York: Routledge, 2013.

I. Glenn Cohen, ed. — *The Globalization of Health Care: Legal and Ethical Issues.* New York: Oxford University Press, 2013.

Dena S. Davis — *Genetic Dilemmas: Reproductive Technology, Parental Choices, and Children's Futures.* New York: Oxford University Press, 2010.

Kenneth W. Goodman, ed. — *The Case of Terri Schiavo: Ethics, Politics, and Death in the 21st Century.* New York: Oxford University Press, 2010.

John Harris — *Enhancing Evolution: The Ethical Case for Making Better People.* Princeton, NJ: Princeton University Press, 2010.

Matti Häyry — *Rationality and the Genetic Challenge: Making People Better?* New York: Cambridge University Press, 2010.

Christopher Kaczor — *The Ethics of Abortion: Women's Rights, Human Life, and the Question of Justice.* New York: Routledge, 2011.

Anja J. Karnein · *A Theory of Unborn Life: From Abortion to Genetic Manipulation.* New York: Oxford University Press, 2012.

Tom Koch · *Thieves of Virtue: When Bioethics Stole Medicine.* Cambridge, MA: MIT Press, 2012.

Calum MacKellar and Christopher Bechtel, eds. · *The Ethics of the New Eugenics.* New York: Berghahn Books, 2014.

Ronald L. Sandler, ed. · *Ethics and Emerging Technologies.* New York: Palgrave Macmillan, 2013.

James D. Slack · *Abortion, Execution, and the Consequences of Taking Life.* New Brunswick, NJ: Transaction Publishers, 2011.

Bonnie Steinbock · *Life Before Birth: The Moral and Legal Status of Embryos and Fetuses.* New York: Oxford University Press, 2011.

Stefan Timmermans and Mara Buchbinder · *Saving Babies?: The Consequences of Newborn Genetic Screening.* Chicago: University of Chicago Press, 2013.

Lewis Vaughn · *Bioethics: Principles, Issues, and Cases.* New York: Oxford University Press, 2013.

Robert M. Veatch · *Hippocratic, Religious, and Secular Medical Ethics: The Points of Conflict.* Washington, DC: Georgetown University Press, 2012.

Periodicals and Internet Sources

Alex B. Berezow	"We Should Approve 'Three-Parent' Embryos," *Real Clear Science*, July 29, 2013. www.realclearscience.com.
James L. Bernat	"Life or Death for the Dead-Donor Rule?," *New England Journal of Medicine*, vol. 369, no. 14, October 3, 2013.
Daniel Callahan and Peter Augustine Lawler	"Ethics and Health Care: Rethinking End-of-Life Care," The Heritage Foundation, July 24, 2012. www.heritage.org.
Philip Caper	"Should Health Care Be Rationed? It Already Is," *Bangor Daily News*, May 15, 2014.
Joe Carter	"38 Ways to Make a Baby," *First Things*, September 28, 2011. www.firstthings.com.
Frank C. Chaten	"The Dead Donor Rule: Effect on the Virtuous Practice of Medicine," *Journal of Medical Ethics*, vol. 40, no. 7, 2014.
Marcia Clark and William Travis Clark	"Selling Your Organs: Should It Be Legal? Do You Own Yourself?," *Forbes*, June 13, 2013.
Marcy Darnovsky and Alexandra Minna Stern	"The Bleak New World of Prenatal Genetics," *Wall Street Journal*, June 12, 2013.

Chuck Donovan	"Obamacare and the Ethics of Life: Weakening Medical Conscience and the Protection of Life," The Heritage Foundation, January 19, 2011. www.heritage.org.
Kevin Drum	"Bring On the Designer Babies," *Mother Jones*, February 26, 2014. www.motherjones.com.
Susan G. Drummond	"Age and Assisted Reproduction," *Toronto Star*, May 6, 2013.
George Erickson	"Single-Payer Health Care Is the Moral Thing to Do," *Duluth News Tribune*, January 17, 2014.
Adam Gaffney	"'Private Option' Won't Help Poor," *USA Today*, July 7, 2014.
Harold Gershowitz and Amy Gershowitz Lask	"Our Deeply Unethical National Organ Policy," *American*, July 7, 2010. www.american.com.
Anthony Gregory	"Why Legalizing Organ Sales Would Help to Save Lives, End Violence," *Atlantic*, November 9, 2011.
David Cay Johnston	"The Myth of Health Care's Free Market," *Newsweek*, January 2, 2014. www.newsweek.com.
Amy Klein	"Embryo Testing Should Not Be Controversial," *Slate*, March 18, 2014. www.slate.com.
Annie Lowrey	"The Kidney Trade," *Slate*, December 15, 2010. www.slate.com.

Alexis C. Madrigal — "Making Babies," *Atlantic*, June 2014.

Samuel Metz — "What the US Really Needs Is a Single-Payer Health System," *Oregonian*, March 17, 2014.

Lawrence Nelson and Brandon Ashby — "Rethinking the Ethics of Physician Participation in Lethal Injection Execution," *Hastings Center Report*, vol. 41, no. 3, May/June 2011. www.thehastingscenter.org.

Sally C. Pipes — "The False Promise of Single-Payer Healthcare," *New York Post*, April 16, 2014.

Fred Rotondaro and Christopher J. Hale — "After *Hobby Lobby*: A Single-Payer Health Care Solution?," *Time*, July 3, 2014.

Daniel B. Rubin — "A Role for Moral Vision in Public Health," *Hastings Center Report*, vol. 40, no. 6, 2010. www.thehastingscenter.org.

Cathy Ruse — "Not Dead Yet: The Fight Over 'Death' in Organ Transplantation," *National Review Online*, September 22, 2011. www.nationalreview.com.

Wesley J. Smith — "The Ethics of Food and Drink," *Weekly Standard*, vol. 19, no. 43, July 28, 2014.

Kim Tingley — "The Brave New World of Three-Parent I.V.F.," *New York Times Magazine*, June 29, 2014.

| Walter E. Williams | "Unnecessary Tragedy," Townhall.com, June 12, 2013. http://townhall.com. |

Index

A

Abortion
    ethical issues around, 42, 115
    integration into primary care,
      166–172
    physician right to perform, 17
    politics of, 166–168
    primary care clinicians and,
      168–170
Acosta, Javier, 61
Advanced practice clinicians
  (APCs), 168–172
Affordable Care Act (ACA)
    declining disapproval of,
      20–22
    financing of, 31–32, 35
    overview, 44
    Republican demand for re-
      peal, 36–37, 39
    RFRA and, 56
    as solution, 38–39
African Americans, 71, 153, 155
Allott, Daniel, 124–131
Alper, Ty, 162–165
American Cancer Society, 29
American College of Obstetricians
  and Gynecologists (ACOG), 126,
  184–187
American Medical Association
  (AMA), 17, 115, 162, 179–180
Americans United for Separation
  of Church and State, 57
Anonymous Father's Day
  (documentary), 138
Anti-conscience movement, 174–
  176
Antidepressant objections, 57

Artificial contraception, 42
Assisted reproduction technologies
  (ART)
    bioethical responsibility, 42,
      108–109
    commercialization of fertility,
      109–111
    concerns over, 124–131
    controversies about, 105–106,
      141–142
    overview, 104–105
    prenatal genetic screening,
      112–116
    risks and benefits, 106–108
    social controversy, 104–111
    surrogate mothers, 121–123
    as unethical, 146–149
Atlanta Journal Constitution
  (newspaper), 181
Autonomy principle, 93

B

Bailey, Ashley, 61–62
Bailey, Ronald, 112–116
Barry, Bruce, 27
Baylor College, 114
Becker, Gary S., 74–81
Berezow, Alex, 133, 134
Biliary atresia, 61–62
Bisset, Mackenzie, 182
Black market donation of organs,
  84
Blood transfusion objections, 57
Brain death, 86–87, 92
Breeders (documentary), 138–145
Brigham and Women's Hospital,
  115

O

P